THE
IMPEACHMENT
DIARY

Also by James Reston, Jr.

To Defend, To Destroy: A Novel, 1971

The Amnesty of John David Herndon, 1973

The Knock at Midnight: A Novel, 1975

The Innocence of Joan Little: A Southern Mystery, 1977

Our Father Who Art in Hell: The Life and Death of Jim Jones, 1981

Sherman's March and Vietnam, 1987

The Lone Star: The Life of John Connally, 1989

*Collision at Home Plate: The Lives of Pete Rose
and Bart Giamatti*, 1991

Galileo: A Life, 1994

The Last Apocalypse: Europe at the Year 1000 A.D., 1998

*Warriors of God: Richard the Lionheart and Saladin
in the Third Crusade*, 2001

*Dogs of God: Columbus, the Inquisition,
and the Defeat of the Moors*, 2005

Fragile Innocence: A Father's Memoir of His Daughter's Courageous Journey, 2006

The Conviction of Richard Nixon: The Untold Story of the Frost/Nixon Interviews, 2007

Defenders of the Faith: Christianity and Islam Battle for the Soul of Europe, 2009

The Accidental Victim: JFK, Lee Harvey Oswald, and the Real Target in Dallas, 2013

Luther's Fortress: Martin Luther and His Reformation Under Siege, 2015

A Rift in the Earth: Art, Memory, and the Fight for a Vietnam War Memorial, 2018

THE IMPEACHMENT DIARY

EYEWITNESS TO THE
REMOVAL OF A PRESIDENT

JAMES RESTON, JR.

With an Introduction by
WALTER DELLINGER

Arcade Publishing • New York

First Edition

Arcade Publishing books may be purchased in bulk at special
discounts for sales promotion, corporate gifts, fund-raising, or
educational purposes. Special editions can also be created to
specifications. For details, contact the Special Sales Department,
Arcade Publishing, 307 West 36th Street, 11th Floor, New York,
NY 10018 or arcade@skyhorsepublishing.com.

Arcade Publishing® is a registered trademark of Skyhorse
Publishing, Inc.®, a Delaware corporation.

Visit our website at www.arcadepub.com.
Visit the author's site at www.restonbooks.com.

10 9 8 7 6 5 4 3 2 1

Library of Congress Cataloging-in-Publication Data is available on file.
Library of Congress Control Number: 2019944455

Cover design by Brian Peterson
Cover photo: Getty Images

ISBN: 978-1-950691-18-0
Ebook ISBN: 978-1-950691-19-7

Printed in the United States of America

For Henry Mayer and Myron Simmons
In Memoriam

Contents

Contents

Preface

WITH THE FIRING OF FBI DIRECTOR James Comey in May 2017, just as with the firing of Special Prosecutor Archibald Cox in October 1973 in the so-called Saturday Night Massacre, the talk of impeaching the president of the United States became serious and widespread in America. Impeachment, that grand constitutional inquest of the nation against the nation's leader, has been a subject of long and intense interest to me ever since the 1970s, when I was deeply involved with addressing the misdeeds of Richard Nixon, first as an observer of the famous Senate Select Committee on Presidential Campaign Activities in the summer of 1973, when the White House tapes were revealed, then as a witness to the final six weeks of the Nixon presidency in the summer of 1974, and finally, as David Frost's Watergate adviser for the renowned *Nixon Interviews* in 1977.

Thirty years later, my account of those historic interviews, titled *The Conviction of Richard Nixon*, was to form the basis for the award-winning play and movie *Frost/Nixon*. The interviews were historic because they forced Nixon, three years after he was driven from office, to acknowledge his criminality and apologize to the nation, and partly because, with an audience of an estimated 47 million viewers, the series remains the most watched public affairs program in the history of American television.

As talk of Donald Trump's obstruction of justice, abuse of power, and defiance of subpoenas grew louder after Comey's firing, with the cascading scandals and crises of the Trump White House, and with the appointment of the new special counsel, Robert Swan Mueller III, I experienced an unexpected sense of déjà vu. Was the country really headed for another formal impeachment proceeding? If we were going down that road, what were the chances of success, if by success was meant the removal of a president from office? And did the country—and its politicians—appreciate the high hurdles that would have to be surmounted before either removal or a presidential resignation could happen?

It is the Nixon experience, not the flawed and discredited effort to remove President Bill Clinton in 1998, that is the template for a process against Donald Trump. Richard Nixon remains the only president in American history who was ever driven from office for high crimes and misdemeanors, crimes that were committed in the sacred space of the Oval Office itself. To know and understand how events unfolded in 1973–1974 is imperative for anyone who wishes to judge the viability of any serious impeachment effort against Trump. Those long-ago events are the measuring stick for the impeachment politics of today.

The formal process against Nixon began on February 6, 1974, when the full US House of Representatives passed a resolution by a vote of 410 to 4 to authorize the House Judiciary Committee to investigate impeachment charges against the president. In four full months of research and investigation, the Judiciary Committee considered 650 "statements of information" and more than 7,200 pages of evidence and interviewed nine witnesses. In June of that year, the committee began its first public hearings. Three impeachment articles eventually passed the committee, with a handful of Republican committee members voting for them and against their party's president. In the US Supreme Court, Nixon would lose in his effort to assert executive privilege and withhold incriminating tape recordings from Congress. The vote against him was unanimous, 8–0. Only with the revelation of the so-called "smoking gun" tape, definitively revealing Nixon's abuse of power, and the defection of many Republicans from his cause, was his fate sealed.

It could have gone differently. Despite overwhelming evidence of the president's wrongdoing, Republicans might have stuck with their man without defection, as they did during the summer of 2019 in the preliminary stage of a possible proceeding against Donald Trump. The vote in the Supreme Court might have been less than unanimous, encouraging Nixon to fight on. A vote in a Senate trial of the president, if it came to that, might have fallen short of the two-thirds supermajority that is required under the Constitution for conviction and removal, as it did fall short in both the impeachment trial of Andrew Johnson in 1868 and of Bill Clinton in 1998. Of course, Nixon resigned after the smoking gun tape was revealed, before the full House of Representatives could formally impeach him and send his case to the Senate for trial. But out of sheer spite, he could have remained in office and dared the Congress and the country to suffer through a six-month impeachment trial in the Senate, as his daughter Julie was urging. In addressing the parallel between the Nixon case and his own on June 10, 2019, President Trump cited one critical difference. "He left. I don't leave."

During the summers of 1973 and 1974, I witnessed this grinding prosecution firsthand, as I worked with Frank Mankiewicz on a book called *Perfectly Clear: Nixon from Whittier to Watergate*. During those last heady six weeks of the Nixon presidency, in 1974, I shuttled between the Watergate trials of top Nixon aides, the House Judiciary Committee hearings, the White House, and the Supreme Court. It was an exciting, dramatic time. History was in the making, and probably, I thought at the time, American history would never again witness another such spectacle, at least not in my lifetime.

I decided to write a diary. No matter how it turned out, I was sure the drama would be worth remembering. And it is. When I unearthed the diary in my papers in the fall of 2018, I was astonished at its relevance to the current situation. In fraught personal detail, it describes the step-by-step process that ended a presidency. Anguishing it may have been, but the journey was necessary and dignified. In the summer of 2019 we heard a lot about how an impeachment process would be "divisive." In 1974 it was ultimately not so divisive as healing, an imperative, if wrenching, catharsis after so much shocking abuse in the Oval Office itself. This was, and is, the road map. It should be read metaphorically. Read Nixon and imagine Trump.

This is how it felt in the summer of 1974.

My model for the diary came from an unlikely source. It was the diary of the young Georges Clemenceau, famous later as the French premier who became known as Tiger of Europe during World War I. Little known is the fact that as a young man, just about my age of thirty-three years in 1974, he lived in Washington, from 1865 to 1869, and wrote dispatches on the impeachment of Andrew Johnson for the radical Paris daily *Le*

Temps. I imagined myself channeling Clemenceau, fantasizing that I was his alter ego: two young, passionate, opinionated observers lucky enough to witness a seminal history moment close up.

I admired and envied Clemenceau for his impeachment. The issue of reconciliation versus reconstruction of the nation after the cataclysm of the American Civil War gripped the nation. Should the Union be restored as it was, with the exception of slavery, as quickly and painlessly as possible? That was Andrew Johnson's view. Or was the South to be fundamentally and harshly reconstructed, with its aristocracy disgraced and impoverished and its former slaves in the ascendancy? That was the view of the Radical Congress and its larger-than-life figures like Thaddeus Stevens, wizened and dying, pressing revolutionary legislation like the Reconstruction Acts and the 14th Amendment, and Charles Sumner, his ally in the Senate, scarred from the brutal caning attack by a Southern congressman twelve years before. Andrew Johnson was caught up in the maelstrom.

Clemenceau's impeachment seemed so much more elevating than mine. The flamboyant politicians he wrote about did not have to consult the latest polls or receive partisan "talking points" to discover what positions to espouse. Even his villain seemed more interesting—my taste runs more to bullheadedness than deviousness. Insult was a better art form in those days. Routinely, the censors had to delete Stevens's expletives from the official record in the *Congressional Globe*. Thaddeus Stevens called Andrew Johnson "the nightmare that crouches upon the heaving breast of the nation" and a "double-skinned rhinoceros." Once, when he was upbraided for his "foul language" in the House, Stevens replied, "That gentleman has complained that my language was foul and talked about it being learned in Billingsgate, Cripplegate, and Newgate [a British fish market, a sheltering place for cripples, and a jail]. Sir, with all the gates that the gentleman has gone through and that he refers to, there is one gate which the gentleman will enter which I shall try to avoid."

My "gate" was Watergate. I had only the banality of its taped evidence, the petty and stupid break-in at the Watergate Hotel, and Nixon the "imperial president," who foolishly authorized the cover-up as he was about to win reelection, with forty-nine out of fifty states voting for him. Who, I wondered as I began my diary, would be my counterparts? Would there be eloquence and wisdom or only cant and shouting? Would I witness courage or cravenness? Never mind, I thought. This would be the best impeachment drama I'd ever get.

Clemenceau had titled his diary *American Reconstruction*. In 1974, after the end of the Vietnam War, the catharsis of Watergate, and the impeachment proceedings, I was hoping for a second American Reconstruction. In coming years, if there is a cleansing impeachment proceeding against Donald Trump, the nation might need the revival of a third Reconstruction.

Georges Clemenceau in 1864.

Introduction

by Walter Dellinger

IN THE SUMMER OF 1974, JAMES RESTON, JR., became an eye-witness to history. As the nation's attention was riveted by the spectacle of a deadly serious presidential impeachment process, Jim dashed from venue to venue—the Congress, the criminal courthouse, the Supreme Court, the White House press room—to record firsthand his view of the unfold-ing drama of the demise of Richard Nixon's presidency. The "impeachment diary" he kept from the end of June until the days of August has now become an extraordinarily valuable guide both to our present moment and to the future of the impeachment process.

Half a century after our days as friends at the University of North Carolina, our mutual interest in presidential impeachments—for Jim as the author of this gripping diary, and for me as a sometime constitutional scholar—has brought us together. I'm honored to provide some context to Jim's work.

After Jim finished college and served in the military, he began his career as a writer and as a creative writing instructor at UNC-Chapel Hill. As luck would have it, he was working on a writing project in Washington during that fateful summer.

He switched his efforts to keeping a chronicle of the impeachment of President Richard Nixon.

The diary he kept that summer was preserved in his attic. And fortunate that is for us, his readers. That work, published here, is entertaining as a page-turning saga. But it is more than that. This account of the only time in American history that a president was forced from office by the impeachment process teaches us valuable lessons about how the impeachment process can work—and how it might not work.

Reston's diary of the Nixon impeachment is being published at a time when impeachment is in the air. The White House is occupied by a president with singular disdain for the rule of law. Some have reached a premature judgment that impeachment of this current president seems unlikely. But one of the lessons of Jim's diary is that one cannot know what will happen with an impeachment process even a few months down the road.

Even if the present term of Donald J. Trump were to expire before impeachment and removal could be completed, the distinct possibility remains that he might be sworn in for a second term beginning in January of 2021. Knowing his capacity for violating his oath of office and for disregarding the law should lead every American to learn as much as possible about the process of impeachment and its history. And if we were to witness a failed impeachment process for the forty-fifth president, we need to understand why it failed—and what we can learn from the successful process by which Richard Nixon was removed from office.

The question of what to do with a lawless president is one of the most perplexing a constitutional democracy can face. It involves a balance between the competing considerations of insuring a vigorous chief executive while also providing protection against the harm a rogue president might do to the country.

The Framers of the Constitution sought to provide each president with a secure term in office and some independence in administering the government. As the constitutional convention in Philadelphia continued its deliberations in the summer of 1787, it became clear that the new federal government they were establishing would be entrusted with sweeping powers. To run such a government, energy in the executive would be required. Thus, early proposals to have the president chosen by Congress and removable whenever Congress found him to have engaged in "maladministration" or "neglect of duty" were rejected as unduly weakening the office of the president. Such close control of the executive by the legislature threatened to cripple the presidency and deprive these newly united states of the vigorous leadership needed to tame a continent and build a nation.

The Framers also rejected the idea of leaving the removal question to the popular vote in the next election. The Framers settled on an impeachment process that was deliberately difficult, however. The Constitution provides scant guidance about the standard for impeaching and removing a president. It tells us only that:

> The President, Vice President and all civil Officers of the United States, shall be removed from Office on Impeachment for, and Conviction of, Treason, Bribery, or other High Crimes and Misdemeanors.

The responsibilities for carrying out this mandate are divided between the House of Representatives and the Senate:

> The House of Representatives . . . shall have the sole Power of Impeachment

which essentially means the power to bring charges against a president of having committed "treason, bribery, or other high crimes and misdeameanors." The Senate's role is set out as follows:

> The Senate shall have the sole Power to try all Impeachments. . . . When the President of the United States is tried, the Chief Justice shall preside: And no Person shall be convicted without the Concurrence of two thirds of the Members present.

Finally, the Constitution provides that:

> Judgment in Cases of impeachment shall not extend further than to removal from Office, and disqualification to hold and enjoy any Office of honor, Trust or Profit under the United States: but the Party convicted shall nevertheless be liable and subject to Indictment, Trial, Judgment and Punishment, according to Law.

The requirement that a president may be removed from office only by a two-thirds vote is a high standard, and rightly so. It was intended to require a clear, and almost always bipartisan, consensus before an elected president is removed from office.

Impeachment and removal by conviction in the Senate is not necessarily the only remedy against a president. A person who was injured by a president could bring a suit for money damages against him in his private capacity. In the case of *Clinton v. Jones*, the Supreme Court unanimously rejected President William Clinton's argument that any private civil actions against a president should be postponed until he is no longer in office. The Court held that even if defending such a suit would be burdensome for the president and could hamper his ability to execute his duties, the plaintiff Paula Jones was nonetheless entitled to have her case against Clinton proceed. (I was on the losing side, arguing as acting solicitor general on behalf of the United States in favor of postponing litigation while a president was in office.) President Trump is currently being sued in state court by an alleged former sexual partner who claims he falsely disparaged her by denying her claims.

What about bringing criminal prosecution against a sitting president who has violated the law? It is clear to almost everyone that you could not force a president to undergo an actual criminal trial while being responsible for the entire executive branch of the national government. But why not, when warranted, allow the grand jury to issue an indictment, even if further proceedings against a president had to be postponed while he served? I would have thought that the decision in *Clinton v. Jones* would mean that a president could be indicted if a federal prosecutor convinced a grand jury that he had committed one or more federal felonies. The Justice Department's Office of Legal Counsel (OLC), however, concluded differently and in an opinion issued at the end of the Clinton administration, in 2000, held that the mere fact of an indictment would "cast a cloud" over the presidency and thus should be precluded.

Having led the OLC from 1993 to 1996, I have great respect for that office's professionalism. However, I disagree with the office's conclusion that even indicting a sitting president is barred. There is nothing in the text of the Constitution or judicial precedent that creates a categorical bar to the indictment of a sitting president. Issuing an indictment against a president, even if no trial could proceed while he remained in office, would bring clarity to the conclusions reached by a special counsel or other prosecutor. Moreover, the issuance of an indictment would ensure that any prosecution was not barred by the "statute of limitations." Most federal crimes must be charged by indictment within five years of commission or be forever barred. If a president can't be indicted while in office, he or she would have a perverse incentive to run for reelection just to ensure that crimes committed in his first term or earlier could never be charged.

I believe it is wrong to make the White House a sanctuary from justice. But opinions of the Office of Legal Counsel are binding on the executive branch unless and until overruled by the Office or by a future attorney general. And that is not likely to happen.

Which brings us back to the difficult and troublesome remedy of impeachment. Here is where Reston's book is a valuable guide. Three times in American history, the impeachment process has been seriously undertaken against a president. Once was in the aftermath of the Civil War. The House's charges against Andrew Johnson, in essence for defying Congress and undermining Reconstruction of the South, ended in his acquittal in the Senate by a single vote. The House's impeachment of

Walter Dellinger testifying before the House Judiciary
Committee. *Photo by Scott J. Ferrell/Congressional Quarterly/
Getty Images*

President Clinton for lying in a federal court proceeding and obstructing justice arising out of his sexual relationship with a White House intern similarly ended in acquittal when the Senate failed to muster a two-thirds vote.

But the impeachment process that is most instructive for our time is the one that resulted in the extraordinary resignation of President Nixon for his role in the Watergate scandal: the cover-up of the break-in of the Democratic Party headquarters and related attempts to subvert the 1972 election. The Nixon example shows how quickly calculations can change. This is another of the diary's lessons. President Nixon had won forty-nine states in the 1972 election. Many thought even well into 1974 that because of this electoral victory he would never be impeached. Even in the summer of 1974, the Nixon impeachment talk was in the doldrums. In a July 15, 1974, entry in the diary, Jim listens to the highly respected *Los Angeles Times* correspondent Jack Nelson speak of how tired both he and the country were of the whole impeachment drama.

This notion that the country was tired of the Watergate investigation held true even though by that time incriminating Oval Office tape records released to the public on July 10 included such memorable quotes as Nixon saying, "I don't give a shit what happens. I want you all to stonewall it. . . . Let them plead the Fifth Amendment . . . cover up or anything else, if it'll save it . . . save the plan." Less than a month later he was gone from office.

As Jim's diary reminds us, narrowly partisan calculations can change, too. Republicans staunchly defended Nixon as the leader of their party almost to the bitter end, as Republicans in Congress are doing now for their partisan leader. Yet, during the proceedings of the House Judiciary Committee as it considered impeachment and eventually voted to send three of five proposed articles of impeachment to the full House for approval, several Republican congressmen broke with the party line to vote their conscience. Many more Republicans broke ranks after the release of the "smoking gun" tape, but even then Nixon still had enough defenders in Congress to weigh the odds of a Senate trial.

David French, writing in *Vanity Fair*, sharply noted the similarities between the Nixon scandal and the investigations into President Trump: "With its bursting cast—whether flawed, ridiculous, conniving, or just evil—and improbable plot, as well as the highest possible stakes, the current DC drama is actually a Watergate sequel." At a more profound level, both the Nixon and Trump investigations involved attempts to subvert democracy itself.

Unfortunately, the investigations into President Trump's misdeeds were marred by missteps in the beginning. First, the special counsel appointed to investigate Russian interference in the 2016 election, Robert Mueller, decided to expand upon the 2000 Office of Legal Counsel opinion. The OLC opinion held that an indictment could not issue against the president while he was in office. It did not address the question of whether the special counsel could report his conclusion that the president had committed crimes. Special Counsel Mueller added that extension, arguing that it would be unfair to the president for a prosecutor to state that the president had committed crimes when the president would not be in a position to go to trial and defend himself. This in my view ignores the fact, first, that the president is in the unique position of enjoying this temporal immunity from indictment and, second, has the world's greatest megaphone for defending himself.

The notion that the special counsel could neither indict nor even express a conclusion that the president had engaged in multiple counts of obstruction of justice led the counsel's report to engage in a confusing double-negative assertion that it could not conclude that the president did not obstruct justice.

The consequences of this voluntary restraint by the Special Counsel were magnified by the overly cautious initial response of the House of Representatives majority to the special counsel's determinations. When the *Mueller Report* was released to the public, President Trump and his defenders immediately claimed that the *Report* was a vindication, and the Democratic House acted as if it were inconclusive. Those responses, one mendacious, one tepid, and both erroneous, threatened to distort public understanding. They not only allowed the president falsely to claim vindication but have left the public without a clear understanding of just how damning the *Report* was.

The House majority initially stated a need to see the redacted portion of the *Report* and to hear from witnesses before drawing any conclusions. This approach was wrong. Mueller's extraordinary 2,500-subpoena, 500–search warrant, two-year investigation fully established not merely crimes but the betrayal of the president's office: a failure to defend the country's electoral system from foreign attack, and acts of interference with justice that shred the rule of law. Congress did not need to read more to announce what was obvious from what it should have read already.

What is important in an impeachment process is for each institution to do its duty, and to do so with a high degree of fealty to law, not politics. One error that can be made is for the House to abstain from doing its duty based on a prediction that two-thirds of a Senate controlled by the president's party would never vote to convict. As we see from Reston's diary, it is impossible to predict how a justly initiated impeachment process will unfold. And if the Senate were to refuse to do its duty of providing an honest trial, so be it. That does not excuse the House from carrying out its own responsibilities. If the House, acting as the "grand inquest of the nation," were to conclude and formally vote that a president had committed "high crimes and misdeameanors," that action by itself could serve history and fulfill each representative's duty to his or her oath of office.

As with a grand jury proceeding, the work of the House Judiciary Committee in deliberating over impeachment can serve to bring clarity to a complex array of alleged acts of misconduct by a president. In ascertaining the facts, then weighing what acts are impeachable, and finally crafting charges into articles susceptible to approval first by the committee and then by a majority in the House, members must sharpen their arguments, work through their own particular partisan opinions, and reckon with their conscience and oath of office to defend the Constitution. The debate over the articles of impeachment against President Nixon served to educate the public, as did the release by the committee of thousands of pages of evidence once the articles of impeachment had been fashioned and were ready to be published.

Finally, I want to note the pleasures to be found in Jim's diary. As a young law professor, I followed Watergate as closely as I could from Duke University. But before reading Jim's diary, I had no sense of the "feel" of those historic final weeks. With ingenuity and energy, Jim managed to worm his way into each of the venues in which this drama was

simultaneously unfolding. First, he would be in the House
Judiciary Committee's hearing room, where the solemn
debate over proposed articles of impeachment was progress-
ing. At the same time, an important criminal trial was taking place. A gang doing the bidding of Nixon's chief aide had
broken into the office of a psychiatrist, hoping to find damaging information against the leaker of the Pentagon Papers.
Jim, working his way into the back of the courtroom, provides vivid descriptions of Judge Gerhard Gesell (who would
unsettle witnesses by never looking at them) and of the criminal defendants, some reprehensibly arrogant like Nixon's aide
John Ehrlichman, some colorful like break-in operative G.
Gordon Liddy.

One gets a feel for the mood of the nation's capital as Jim
describes what he sees as he goes about the quotidian tasks of
everyday life. Going to get his car washed, "out of curiosity I
drove by the Supreme Court to take in scene" the afternoon
before the historic argument in *United States v. Nixon*, the case
that would determine whether the president could be com-
pelled to turn over incriminating tape recordings. Jim sees
already forty people in sleeping bags hoping to get inside the
courtroom the next morning. Jogging later, he sees the crowd
swell. Only a contemporaneous diary can convey the intensity
and, finally, exhilaration of those days in the summer of 1974.

Jim at one point becomes a participant and not just an
observer of this drama. His efforts provide us with another
of the lessons useful for our time. From the earliest days of
his diary, Jim expressed concern that those seeking Nixon's
removal would fall into a trap set by the President's defenders,
who sought to "narrow the issue to one conclusive criminal
act." Jim understood that an impeachable offense need not be

limited to those acts that meet each element of a crime under the federal criminal code.

Such a limitation would not capture clear violations of a president's oath of office as a deliberate refusal to defend the United States against foreign attack (including, in our time, a foreign military intelligence attack on our election system). In the summer of 2019, it became evident from the *Mueller Report* and the report of a bipartisan Senate Select Committee on Intelligence that President Trump had engaged in that very behavior.

Jim sought to counter the emerging narrow focus on possible specific crimes by Nixon by submitting an op-ed to the *Washington Post* (which has been reprinted as an appendix to this book). He was pessimistic about its chances for acceptance, noting that there were said to be about eight hundred journalists "hovering over this spectacle." Jim, not then the acclaimed author of many award-winning books as he is today, could only offer the identification of "author and lecturer in creative writing" at UNC. Readers of the diary will experience Jim's youthful joy when the *Post* editor calls with the news that the paper would indeed publish his piece and his renewed joy seeing his essay in the paper "in all its glory." Jim's proposal that there should be an "omnibus impeachment article that would encompass the entire case against Nixon in one sweeping statement" was partially successful, as the final articles of impeachment against Nixon made large assertions with particular specifications.

Now, as then, many responsible voices are saying that pursuing impeachment against a president should be avoided because the proceedings could prove to be divisive. Jim Reston's *Impeachment Diary* suggests a different conclusion.

He wrote of the Nixon impeachment process that "In 1974 it was ultimately not so divisive as healing, an imperative, if wrenching, catharsis after so much shocking abuse in the Oval Office itself."

We would do well to take heed of those words now and in the future.

Walter Dellinger is the Douglas B. Maggs Emeritus Professor of Law at Duke University and a Washington, DC, attorney. He served as assistant attorney general of the United States and head of the Office of Legal Counsel from 1993 to 1996 and acting solicitor general of the United States from 1996 to 1997.

James Reston, Jr., in the summer of 1974. *Sally F. Reston*

Dramatis Personae
(in order of appearance)

James "Sam" Ervin: US senator from North Carolina, 1954–1974, and chairman of the Select Committee on Presidential Campaign Activities, also known as the Senate Watergate Committee, 1973–1974.

Georges Clemenceau: Future prime minister of France during World War I, who as a young man witnessed the impeachment proceedings against Andrew Johnson and wrote essays for the Paris journal *Le Temps* from 1865 to 1868. His diary of the impeachment is published in the book *American Reconstruction*.

Howard Baker: US senator, 1966–1985. A moderate who was the first Republican senator from Tennessee since Reconstruction. Known as the Great Conciliator for his skill at compromise, he served as both Senate Majority and Minority leader, and later became the US ambassador to Japan. In Watergate lore, he is best known for his defining question, "What did the president know, and when did he know it?"

John Dean: White House counsel to President Nixon, July 1970 to April 1973. FBI dubbed him "the master manipulator" of the Watergate cover-up. His conversation with the president on March 21, 1973, in which he described a "cancer on the presidency," became a critical piece of evidence against Nixon in both the Select Committee and Judiciary Committee hearings. Convicted of a single felony, he served four months in custody.

Charles E. Wiggins: Republican congressman from California, 1967–1979. He became Nixon's chief defender in Congress during the Judiciary Committee impeachment hearings. After the revelation of the "smoking gun" tape in August 1974, he announced that he would vote for the article about Nixon obstructing justice.

James Draper St. Clair: Chief legal counsel for President Nixon who defended the president during the Judiciary Committee hearings and argued for the defense in the case known as *United States vs. Richard Nixon* in the US Supreme Court.

Daniel Ellsberg: Military analyst who leaked the Pentagon Papers, the government study about the failures of the Vietnam War effort, to the *New York Times* and was charged and eventually acquitted under the 1917 Espionage Act. Operatives from the White House broke into the office of his psychiatrist on September 9, 1971, searching for material to discredit Ellsberg. The Ellsberg break-in eventually led to criminal convictions of top White House officials.

Peter W. Rodino, Jr.: Democratic congressman from New Jersey, 1949–1989, who was the chairman of the House Judiciary Committee in June 1974 that voted for three impeachment articles against Nixon.

Gordon Liddy: Former FBI agent and leading figure of the Plumbers unit. He led the team that burglarized the office of Daniel Ellsberg's psychiatrist and later the Watergate office of the Democratic National Committee on June 17, 1972. Convicted of burglary and conspiracy, he refused to testify before the Senate Select Committee. He served four and a half years in federal prison.

Howard Hunt: CIA agent from 1949 to 1970. Along with Gordon Liddy, he was the leader of the Plumbers who planned and carried out the burglary at the Watergate and other secret operations. He was convicted of burglary, conspiracy, and wiretapping and served thirty-three months in prison.

Bernard Barker and Eugenio Martinez: Watergate burglars. Both were veterans of the 1961 Bay of Pigs invasion and worked as undercover agents for the CIA. They were recruited by Howard Hunt for the break-in at Ellsberg's psychiatrist's office in 1971 and the Watergate break-in in 1972.

Charles Colson: Special counsel to the president, known as Nixon's "hatchet man" for his tough talk and aggressive advice. The White House conduit to Hunt and the burglars, he pleaded guilty to obstruction of justice and was the first White House official to go to jail. The author uncovered Nixon-Colson conversations that had the president conspiring to cover up the Watergate burglary on June 20, 1974, three days before the "smoking gun" conversation. Quotes from that conversation were used to good effect in the 1977 *Nixon Interviews* with David Frost.

John Ehrlichman: Chief domestic adviser to President Nixon who created the Plumbers unit. He resigned in April 1973. Tried and convicted of conspiracy, obstruction of justice, and perjury, he served a year and a half in federal prison.

Egil "Bud" Krogh, Jr.: Member of the Plumbers who approved the burglary at the office of Daniel Ellsberg's psychiatrist. He was convicted of conspiring to violate the psychiatrist's civil rights and served four and a half months in prison.

David Young: Originally an assistant in the National Security Council (NSC), he joined the Plumbers unit as a subordinate to Egil Krogh and John Ehrlichman. Granted immunity by the courts, he became the star witness against his superiors in the Ellsberg break-in trial.

Gerhard Gesell: United States District Court judge for the District of Columbia who presided over the various Watergate trials that sent senior White House and Nixon campaign officials including John Ehrlichman, John Mitchell, H. R. Haldeman, and Charles Colson to prison.

James Reston ("Dad"): The author's father, columnist for the *New York Times*.

John Mitchell: US attorney general under Nixon and director of the president's 1972 campaign. Charged with conspiracy, obstruction of justice, and perjury, he served nineteen months in prison.

H. R. Haldeman: Nixon's chief of staff. His conversation with Nixon of June 23, 1974, was the "smoking gun" tape that drove Nixon from office. It revealed abuse of power in which the two conspired to cover up the Watergate break-in. Haldeman was convicted of perjury, conspiracy, and obstruction of justice in the cover-up and served eighteen months in prison.

Leon Jaworski: The second special prosecutor in the Watergate scandal, after the first, Archibald Cox, was fired by Nixon in October 1973 in the so-called Saturday Night Massacre. By prevailing in the US Supreme Court in the Nixon case, Jaworski gained access to sixty-four unedited White House tape recordings that included the "smoking gun" tape of June 23, 1972.

Stewart Udall: Secretary of the interior in the Kennedy and Johnson administrations and brother of Congressman Morris Udall, who ran for president as a Democrat in 1976. The author was an aide to Secretary Udall in 1963–1964.

Charles "Chuck" Morgan, Jr.: Civil rights attorney from Alabama who ran the ACLU legislative office in Washington during the impeachment struggle. He played a pivotal role in the 1964 *Reynolds v. Sims* case that was argued before the Supreme Court and established the precept of "one man, one vote." He also represented Julian Bond and Muhammad Ali in their legal cases.

Baruch Korff: A rabbi and the founder of the National Citizens' Committee for Fairness to the Presidency, a vocal advocacy group in support of Nixon during the president's 1974 troubles. Known as "Nixon's rabbi," Korff pleaded with Nixon not to resign even after the revelation of the "smoking gun" tape.

John Doar: Prominent civil rights lawyer who was appointed as special counsel for the Democratic side in the Judiciary Committee impeachment hearings.

Lawrence Hogan: Republican congressman from Maryland, 1969–1975, who was the first Republican on the House Judiciary Committee to announce that he would vote for the first article of impeachment. He was the only Republican on the committee to vote for all three impeachment articles.

Warren Burger: Chief justice of the United States Supreme Court from 1969 to 1986. He delivered the Court's decision in *United States vs. Richard Nixon* after an 8–0 vote of the justices, ordering the release of sixty-four unedited tapes to the special prosecutor.

Paul "Pete" McCloskey, Jr.: a maverick Republican congressman from California from 1967 to 1983 who ran against Nixon in 1972 on an anti-war platform.

Richard M. Nixon: The thirty-seventh president of the United States. Only five months after the Watergate burglary, with the Watergate cover-up firmly in place, Nixon won reelection in November 1972 with 60 percent of the popular vote, losing only Massachusetts and the District of Columbia. He is the only president in American history to resign from office.

THE
IMPEACHMENT
DIARY

June 22, 1974

It's only three months since my thirty-third birthday, and after giving the university the news that I'll be taking off teaching for a semester, we've finally arrived in Washington from Carolina, flushed with excitement about the months ahead and at being here at such a historic moment. This is certain to be the greatest political drama of our lifetime. We will surely never experience another impeachment of an American president.

What lies ahead is the spectacle of the great American nation exercising the most serious remedy of its Constitution. Last summer, when I was here for the Ervin committee hearings, the public extravaganza was dramatic enough: the revelation of the tapes, John Dean's "cancer on the presidency" testimony, the 18½-minute gap, and the hush-money payments to the burglars. Eighteen top administration figures, including presidential assistants H. R. Haldeman and John Ehrlichman and Attorney General John Mitchell, are facing jail for the cover-up. Presiding over the whole amazing show was courtly, wise, folksy old Senator Sam Ervin, who is surely a great American.

In the final report of the public hearings, I remember how Ervin defined the Watergate scandal as a conglomerate of illegal and unethical activities. But he stressed that his investigation did not undertake to usurp the power of impeachment, which the Constitution confers on the House of Representatives. Characteristically, he left the matter with biblical and literary allusions in his final letter in his committee's final report. He quoted the biblical warning: "*Nothing is covered that shall not be revealed; neither hid that shall not be known. Be not deceived: God is not mocked: For whatsoever a man soweth, that shall he reap.*" He invoked the Roman poet Ennius, "*When crowns are at stake, no friendship is sacred, no faith shall be kept.*" And even Rudyard Kipling from his poem about Tomlinson's ghost, "*For the sin ye do two by two, you must pay for one by one.*"

I witnessed much of it firsthand last summer. But now, this, this! is the final act. It is not to be missed.

We're settled in our turret apartment in a nineteenth-century town house on the corner of 7th and A Streets, SE, that commands a sniper's view up and down these two sleepy streets. We came worried about the safety of the neighborhood, despite its proximity to the Capitol, until we heard the story of a heroic neighbor who witnessed a woman having her purse snatched nearby and who sprang into action after the robber, running him down and returning the purse to the old lady. I've had bookshelves built in my tiny study and set my desk just right to go to work. We sleep on a mattress on the floor, Japanese-style.

In walking distance, there's an old-fashioned drugstore on East Capital Street with a counter, great ice cream, and even egg creams for my Bronx-born wife. Jimmy's on Pennsylvania Avenue features a tasty pasta and bean soup along with sumptuous double-decker sandwiches. Down the street a few doors is the legendary Trover's Book Shop, perfect for browsing and for its stationery supplies in the basement, and in the next block the legendary Vietnam-era dives, Hawk and Dove and

Tune Inn. The other way on the avenue, the Eastern Market beckons on 8th Street. We're bonding with the Greek vegetable and fruit man, Mr. Kalomaris, and the Frenchman with his jaunty beret at the chicken stand with his savory *poulet au pot*.

In the morning, Denise mounts her three-speed Sears bicycle and bikes to her office at the ACLU, where the campaign for Nixon's impeachment is in full swing as her boss, the venerable Charles Morgan, Jr. works with John Doar, the Democratic counsel for the Judiciary Committee. The historic hearings are to begin next week.

I've decided I'm going to write a diary of the coming months. No matter how it all turns out, this will be worth remembering. I will try to be diligent in chronicling my experiences.

June 27, 1974

I am weary of this phrase, "What did the president know and when did he know it?" Ever since Senator Howard Baker uttered those words last summer in the Ervin committee hearings, it has hovered over the investigation like a scarecrow and become the mantra of all sides, it seems. The phrase goes together with the other catchphrase of the day: the search for a "smoking gun." This narrows the debate in this great national inquest to a single event like the March 21 conversation with John Dean about the "cancer on the presidency" when Nixon authorizes hush money to the Watergate burglars. This narrowing ignores the whole sweep of corruption: the Watergate break-in and the cover-up, the abuse of power and obstruction of justice, the Huston Plan, the secret bombing of Cambodia, and Nixon's seedy tax evasions.

A week ago, before the Judiciary Committee's open hearings began, several "persuadable" members—a few Republicans and Southern Democrats—said they recognized the "Wiggins trap," that is, the effort by Congressman Charles Wiggins of California, the president's chief defender in the House, to narrow the issue to one conclusive criminal act.

So yesterday I took an opinion piece over to the *Washington Post*, proposing that in addition to specific, event-based charges, there should be an omnibus impeachment article that would encompass the entire case against Nixon in one sweeping statement. Today, James St. Clair, the president's lawyer, began his presentation to the House Judiciary Committee and launched his defense of the president on the hush-money charge that was paid to the ringleader, Howard Hunt. While many dismiss what he says about Nixon's involvement in this matter, St. Clair will still succeed in focusing attention on that single conversation rather than on the pattern of conduct. Nobody seems to be talking about the larger issue of dereliction of duty anymore.

In the piece, I quote the impeachment inquiry's own staff report on the constitutional grounds for impeachment that was issued five months ago.

"In an impeachment proceeding, a president is called to account for abusing powers that only a president possesses." Whatever happened to that general standard? I suppose it's a long shot that my piece will be taken. There are supposed to be about eight hundred journalists hovering over this spectacle. What authority do I have? My identification for the piece reads: "Author and lecturer in creative writing at the University of North Carolina." In the pile of submissions that the *Post* is surely receiving, I'll be easily dismissed. But if by some miracle they take the piece, perhaps I can force some people to think about the broader charges.

Today, outside the door of the Judiciary Committee, my Chapel Hill classmate and friend, Paul Houston, now a *Los Angeles Times* reporter, told me that Peter Rodino, the Democratic chairman of the Judiciary Committee, had told him, thinking it was in confidence, that he was now sure that all the Democrats would vote for impeachment and expected perhaps five Republicans to do likewise. The chairman wants to have at least that many Republicans so that it "looks good" to the House.

Paul has a difficult problem, since Rodino had been too candid for his own good. He evidently used language like "We've got all the Democrats wrapped up." Paul said he would handle the story as lightly as he could, writing something like "the chairman is known to believe. . . ." Rather than quote him directly. "If we weren't all for impeachment," Paul said, "we'd quote him directly."

I spent most of the afternoon at the US District Courthouse waiting to get into the room as the jury was being empaneled for the Ellsberg break-in case. I've always loved the characterization of the president's private police force as "the Plumbers." How stupid was it, anyway, for a cloak-and-dagger operation to be crafted in the White House to burglarize a psychiatrist's office in the hope of getting damaging information about the hero of the Pentagon Papers? The jury sorted out to be fifteen blacks and only three whites. There's been an assault on Washington juries lately. Presidential defenders like the conservative columnist Patrick Buchanan and Senator Carl Curtis of Nebraska have claimed that juries in Washington don't reflect the American people as a whole. They mean juries here are black and liberal. It's transparent racism, or at least that's what I thought until this afternoon. Now I'm inclined to think that if primarily blacks judge the likes of Ehrlichman, it's only the chickens coming home to roost.

The principals were fascinating to see in the flesh. I particularly wanted to see what Gordon Liddy looks like, and I wasn't disappointed. His skin is blanched white, his black eyes are sunken beneath his thick eyebrows, and his hair and thick brush mustache are carefully manicured. As jury selection proceeded, Liddy's eyes darted back and forth between his legal pad of jury names and the black citizens who paraded to the stand for questioning. Liddy's appearance reminded me of the story about the little alligators who are brought home from Florida by New Yorkers and then flushed down the toilet when they get too big. They live for years in the sewers of New York and grow to be immense and very white.

Ehrlichman, in turn, sported new mod wire-rim glasses and watched with approval as his African American lawyer sought to ingratiate himself to the black jury. Ehrlichman's racist and anti-Semitic remarks are well-known from the tapes.

Poor Bernard Barker and Eugenio Martinez! The real-life burglars. They've already spent eighteen months in jail, and the most that any of their presidential handlers like Charles Colson have spent in the slammer is one year. It's as if they ran the whole operation alone without guidance. I remembered the line I wrote in *Perfectly Clear*: "When all the Watergate evidence is in and all the trials have been held, will only the lowest agents of the conspiracy be the ones with the stiffest sentences?"

Barker, looking a bit like Elmer Fudd, appeared to be confused by the proceeding, his rubbery, deeply tanned Miami skin twitching as he whispered to Martinez. Martinez is strikingly handsome, trim, and athletic for a man of fifty-six years with silver hair. He lives up to his Miami nickname of "*Musculos*" or "Muscles." One couldn't help being impressed at the sight of a guy who has made at least 150 clandestine missions into Cuba during the sixties, and, if one is to believe the rumor, an equal number of politically motivated burglaries, before he was caught in the Big One.

After the session, I called over to their young lawyer, Daniel Schultz, whom I interviewed at length and profitably last summer. I wished him luck. I want Barker and Martinez released and free to live a quiet life for the rest of their years in southwest Miami, while I hope Ehrlichman gets the max. I don't care what happens to Liddy.

And it appears nobody else does either. In the edited transcript of April 14, 1973, tape, there's a discussion about getting word to Liddy that the president's interest is no longer served by Liddy keeping silent:

> **President:** What does Colson want us to do?
> **Ehrlichman:** Several things. He wants you to persuade Liddy to talk.
> **P:** Me? Bring Liddy in and tell him to talk?
> **E:** You can't bring him in. He's in jail.
> **P:** Oh.
> **E:** You would send word to him, of course, through a spokesman.
> **Haldeman:** As Dean points out, he is not talking, 'cause he thinks he's supposed not to talk. If he is supposed to talk, he will. All he needs is a signal, if you want to turn Liddy on.
> **P:** Yeah. But the point . . . that Colson wants to call the signals—is that right?
> **E:** He wants you to be able to say afterward that you cracked the case.

Obviously, the president never turned Liddy on.

June 28, 1974

Hold on! Phillip Geyelin, the editorial director at the *Post*, just called to say that my piece on an omnibus article will run over the weekend! He says my argument comports with the *Post*'s view of the matter and wants me to do more!

And Paul Houston's revelation about Rodino is causing a big flap. The White House is saying that Rodino should be "discharged" as the Judiciary Committee chairman for pre-judging the case. On the floor of the House, Rodino is denying that he said those things to Houston, but ABC News is corroborating the substance of the article.

I attended the opening arguments in the Ellsberg break-in case this morning. Again, I couldn't keep my eyes off Liddy. Today, he looks like a Russian Cossack, and I see him in that scene from *Doctor Zhivago* where the Cossack gallops at full speed toward the stick with a watermelon on it and slices it in half with his cutlass.

The prosecutor, William Merrill, did a precise, yeoman's job of laying out the case. None of the information was especially new to me, except perhaps for the news that Howard Hunt's clandestine camera (which he took to Los Angeles to case Dr. Fielding's office) was concealed in a tobacco pouch. The number of memos filtering to and from Ehrlichman before the break-in also surprised me. That would seem to constitute a solid, documented instance of Ehrlichman's

9

thorough knowledge of the operation. And then this climactic claim: having determined that the break-in is feasible, they call Ehrlichman in Cape Cod.

"It looks all right," his Plumber assistant, Egil Krogh, says.

"Oh, good," Ehrlichman replies, "Let me know if you find anything."

We learn that the burglars brought deliverymen clothes and left a briefcase in Fielding's office while the cleaning ladies were at work. I look at Liddy and try to imagine him in his deliveryman costume. The prosecutor promises to prove a "consciousness of guilt" on Ehrlichman's part after the failed break-in by citing the way the presidential assistant tried to cover his tracks later. In January 1973 Ehrlichman persuades General Robert Cushman, deputy director of the CIA, to write a memo about CIA's help to Hunt and asks him expressly not to include his name in the report. In March of last year, he called another White House operative, David Young, asking him to bring all the documents relating to the case to him. According to the prosecution, Ehrlichman removes a few key documents implicating him in the caper before returning the packet to Young. Consciousness of guilt. Interesting concept.

Ehrlichman's black lawyer, Henry H. Jones, leads off for the defense with character testimony. "There's nothing in this man's background to suggest he could ever violate the Fourth Amendment," he said. The gambit of the defense will be to argue that Ehrlichman did not understand his approval of a "covert" operation to be the approval of a burglary. Jones compares his client's understanding to somebody making a bank deposit, a "confidential action, not to be known, but not illegal." He characterizes Ehrlichman's participation as being only in nominal charge of the Plumbers. Their strategy will be to attack David Young as the prosecution's chief witness. Young is a "rat who was caught in a trap . . . and realized the game was up." He reacted "to save his own neck." So the "blame-your-rogue-subordinate" game, especially if he is your accuser, is in full swing. As for the charge that Ehrlichman lied to the FBI and perjured himself before the grand jury, the lawyer pleads:

"Human fallibility can always explain a loss of memory."

The presentation of Liddy's lawyer is brief and simple. Liddy had presidential authority to undertake the break-in. It was authorized by his superiors. As proof, he cites the May 22, 1973, statement by the president about the formation of the Plumbers unit.

"I did impress upon Mr. Krogh the vital importance to the national security of his assignment," Nixon said. "I did not authorize, and had no knowledge of, any illegal means to be used to achieve this goal. However, because of the emphasis I put on the crucial importance of protecting the national security, I can understand how highly motivated individuals could have felt justified in engaging in specific activities that I would have disapproved, had they been brought to my attention."

Barker's defense lawyer, Dan Schultz, dropped a few bombs in his opening statement. Barker, he posited, undertook three break-ins for the CIA as "training exercises": one in the RKO studios in New York, the other two against anti-Cuban targets in Miami. He also asserted that Barker and Martinez made false representations on their tax returns at the direction of the CIA to disguise where they got their money.

"Breaking these laws," he told the jury, "was all done in performance of work for this government."

I think Schultz is opening the door just a crack here, enough to show that the Cubans were indeed the government's bagmen but not enough to expose them to new charges. It was natural, Schultz argued, that Barker and Martinez, accustomed as they were to secrecy, would not question the operation in Los Angeles.

I come away wondering if this jury will be up to the task. The case is so infinitely complex. Already there's a burly guy in the center of the jury box whose head is beginning to nod forward on his chest.

As I recount this, I remember another of Senator Ervin's literary references in his final statement. In contemplating the motives that inspired their misdeeds, he invoked Cardinal Wolsey's lament in Shakespeare's *Henry VIII*, Act III, Scene 2:

> Had I but serv'd my God with half
> The zeal I serv'd my King,
> He would not in mine age have left me
> Naked to mine enemies.

Senator Sam Ervin. *Library of Congress, Prints & Photographs*

June 30, 1974

How pleasing it was to open the *Washington Post* this morning to see my essay there in all its glory. Now I eagerly await the reaction, if there is one. I can hope for some discussion, at least, of its salient, and I think important, elements, mainly the historical references. Is Georges Clemenceau listening? The debate should now be on what impeachment means, given the confusion on this point out there. The House Judiciary Committee in February made an important distinction. Citing the English roots of our impeachment law in the American Constitution, the report stated that indictable crime cannot be the sole standard for the removal of a president. Criminal law and impeachment are not substitutes for one another and are not interchangeable. Indeed, they have radically different purposes.

"In an impeachment proceeding a President is called to account for abusing powers that only a President has," the report stated.

Instead of concentrating on the second fundamental standard of impeachment, i.e., "serious dereliction of duty," congressmen now seem obsessed with the minute instances of criminal activity, like the March 21 "cancer on the presidency" conversation with John Dean, as if only a single instance of crime will be enough to drive Nixon from office. Is that the most important evidence there is? I ask in the piece, when it took place after nine months of documented cover-up? Impeachment should begin with the Plumbers and the Huston Plan and the Ellsberg break-in, the presidential authorization of illegal wiretapping—now being trivialized as "electronic surveillance"—and of burglary called "surreptitious entry."

Then, nodding to Clemenceau, I pivoted to the eleventh article of impeachment against Andrew Johnson, the all-encompassing omnibus article, crafted by Thaddeus Stevens. As always, his language was colorful. He too groused about how his colleagues were focused on the most trifling crimes and misdemeanors, whereas his final article, encompassing all charges, was "the gist and vital portion of this entire prosecution." He called it "one and a half" of an impeachment article.

"Never was a greater malefactor so gently treated as Andrew Johnson," thundered the Great Emancipator. The president's actions amounted to a "monstrous usurpation worse than sedition and little short of treason." If his comprehensive article was accepted, he said, "what chance has Andrew Johnson to escape, even if all the rest of the articles should fail. Unfortunate man, thus surrounded, hampered, twisted in the meshes of his own wickedness . . . unfortunate, unhappy man, behold your doom!"

God, how I love that antiquated language. But will the notables pay attention to this notion of an omnibus article? Probably not, in these strange times. And anyway, Stevens's article failed by one vote.

July 1, 1974

I returned this afternoon to the Ellsberg break-in trial to hear
the testimony of David Young, the government's star witness
and the man who defined himself as being "co-responsible"
with Egil Krogh for the Plumbers unit. He is balding, trim, and,
of course, well-tailored as if he's a member of the early morning
tennis set in Washington. There's a suggestion of a lisp in his
speech, and his mouth moves nervously, as if after lunch he was
trying to remove food stuck between his back teeth. His eyes
are lazy as he answers, trying hard to appear bored.

He's known as a reluctant witness, and the judge admon-
ished him more than a few times about not being responsive
to the questions. Once, the judge said to the jury: "Speculation
is not evidence" and instructed Young sternly about testifying precisely about who said what and in what order rather
than talking about the "tenor, essence, or substance" of a given
conversation.

In the March 27 taped conversation relating to the prosecution's "consciousness of guilt" theme, Young quoted
Ehrlichman as saying that he had removed the sensitive,
incriminating documents from the file because they showed
"too much forethought." That was the most damaging phrase
of his testimony. Young protested to Ehrlichman, he said,
because he feared "someone else may have copies," knowing
full well that he himself had made Xerox copies of the same

documents. Ehrlichman had replied, "We'll just have to take that chance." At another meeting with his boss, Young remembered saying that he, Young, did not have the authority to order a break-in, and that was why he went to Ehrlichman for authorization in the first place.

"I assumed you had the authority," Young remembered saying, "or you would get it from someone who did."

"You don't want to address yourself to the question of whether I talked to the president about it," Ehrlichman had snapped back.

At the conclusion of the March 27 conversation, Young presented a marvelous analogy. He was like the man sitting in the back of the ambulance, with the president as the driver. He counseled the driver to run the red light, because of the gravity of the patient's condition, which of course, caused an accident at the intersection. Leaving this strained illusion, Young professed still to feel that the Ellsberg problem had required a "presidential decision" and that, given what they were up against at the time—what, in September 1971?!—the decision had been the right one.

The analogy did not quite rise to the heights of head-scratching discombobulation achieved last month during the confirmation hearings of Earl Silbert to be US attorney, when Assistant Attorney General Henry Petersen protested that he had done nothing wrong in keeping the president informed about grand jury actions in the Watergate cases. Said Petersen:

"I'm no whore. I walked through a minefield and came out clean."

The television tonight is saying that Young's testimony was the most damaging yet against Ehrlichman. But the commentator wondered how much impact it would have on the jury, since Young talked in such a monotone that several members of the jury were falling asleep. Still, I have hopes for an alert young jury member on the back row who is eagle-eyed and listens intently.

Oh, I almost forgot. Young, the great phrasemaker, told of the painful talk he had with Ehrlichman on the day his boss resigned. Said Ehrlichman:

"It is better for the president that I resign now. I'll be vindicated in the end, but right now, I'm going to throw a downfield block for the president."

July 2, 1974

I suppose we should grant Mr. Krogh a small measure of sympathy. He at least has acted on his guilt with remorse, an admission of being misguided, and a promise to tell all. At his sentencing, he said:

"I simply feel that what was done in the Ellsberg operation was a violation of what I perceived to be a fundamental idea in this country: the paramount importance of the rights of the individual. I don't want to be associated with that violation any longer by attempting to defend it."

He seems eager to take his share of the blame and face it like a man. There was a faint echo of a more famous confession by a far worse villain, Albert Speer after Nuremberg, who said: "Those who ask me are fundamentally expecting me to offer justifications. But I have none. No apologies are possible."

Krogh has already spent four months in jail after pleading guilty to violating the civil rights of Dr. Fielding. Today on the stand, he stood tall, lean, square-shouldered, and square-jawed, and one might have thought he was testifying about the pro football players' strike that has now begun. Jail seems to have agreed with him. Last week in an interview he gushed about what a good experience jail had been for him. He had learned modern farming methods in the Pennsylvania countryside outside the Lewisburg Federal Prison and was sure that he would never have learned such skills in any other way. He had met many fine people, he said, some of whom he hoped to be friends for the rest of his life. This was in contrast to John Dean's plea bargain, in which he expressed the fear that, with his gentle, boyish appearance, he would be an easy target for abuse in a state prison.

I thought the prosecutor was negligent in not asking Krogh if he understood full well the illegality of a covert entry and if he was not convinced that Ehrlichman also fully understood that. It's likely Merrill will pick up that line of questioning in his redirect examination. He did so with Young. Young's answer was emblematic. "I did not focus on whether or not it was legal or illegal. I focused on the object, which was to examine the Ellsberg files without his consent." Imagine a jewel thief providing such an explanation: "I only focused on stealing the jewels, not whether it was legal or illegal." But Young admitted, "I recognize it as a serious invasion of privacy. I don't know whether I perceived of it as a violation of the law."

A few more memorable moments from today's day in court. As the conspirators learn that Howard Hunt is about to squeal to the prosecutors about the seamy things he did at the White House, Ehrlichman tells Krogh to "hang tight." On the day after the break-in, Ehrlichman calls Krogh in Florida and reveals that he has just been interviewed by the FBI and had to "dissemble." What did that mean? the prosecutor wanted to know.

"To be less than candid" was the answer.

July 3, 1974

This evening President Nixon is on the television from Moscow, seated at a magnificent gilded table in the "green room" of the Kremlin, as he addresses the Russian people over their TV. As he intones, "Just as a cloth is stronger than the thread from which it is made, so the network of agreements we have been weaving is greater than the sum of its parts," I wonder who wrote the speech. The story from Moscow is that the leaders were not able to reach any agreement on nuclear bomb limitations. So the summit was routine. No news, no breakthroughs. What was the point?

"We have been able to meet this year, as we will meet again next year in the United States"—really?—"not in an atmosphere of crisis but rather in an atmosphere of confidence.... The most remarkable thing about this summit meeting is that it is taking place so routinely, so familiarly."

And so the surreal atmosphere continues. A farmer neighbor of ours in the country wants to know how much the Moscow extravaganza is costing the taxpayers. Was it only a show at our expense to divert attention from impeachment? If so, it's not working. The papers carry the routine summit routinely: no headlines and usually second play to actions in the Supreme Court and the Judiciary Committee. All foreign affairs stories seemed to be couched in their relationship to impeachment. Rumors are rife about Nixon's drinking and insomnia. Last fall during the five-day Arab-Israeli War and in the context of his firing the special prosecutor, Archibald Cox, in the Saturday Night Massacre, he was apparently drunk and incapacitated. Only with the firing of Cox did the talk of impeaching Nixon become serious. There's speculation that Kissinger is running foreign policy while Al Haig is the acting president. As Nixon's anti-Semitic remarks on the tapes came out, there were signs in Jerusalem that read "We're all Jew boys here."

In his brief to the Supreme Court two days ago, James St. Clair argued that "the presidency cannot function if the president is preoccupied with the defense of a criminal case." Moscow was supposed to show that Nixon is still functioning. St. Clair went on, "the thought of a president exercising his great powers from a jail cell boggles the mind. The president *is* the executive department." It's doubtful he'll get very far with those arguments. In his reply brief, Leon Jaworski, the special prosecutor, stated that the grand jury had "substantial evidence" of Nixon's involvement in the cover-up when they named him an unindicted co-conspirator.

In sum, there's the feeling of a slow tightening of the noose. The Judiciary Committee, the Supreme Court, the Select Committee report, the Watergate cover-up trial in September—all are bad events for the president.

Yet I catch myself in my overconfidence. Despite all these processes tightening slowly but inexorably, might he still not wriggle out of it? Wriggling is his forte.

I'm reminded of that marvelous passage from Clemenceau, September 10, 1867:

At each session they add a shackle to his bonds, tighten the bit in a different place, file a claw or draw a tooth, and then when he is well bound up, fastened, and caught in the inextricable net of laws and decrees, more or less contradicting each other, they tie him to the stake of the Constitution and take a good look at him, feeling quite sure he cannot move this time. . . . And then Seward, the Dalila of the piece, rises up and shouts: "Johnson, here come the radicals with old Stevens at their head. They are proud of having subjected you and are coming to enjoy the sight of you in chains." And Samson summons all his strength and bursts his cords and bonds with a mighty effort, and the Philistines (I mean the Radicals) flee in disorder to the Capitol to set to work making new laws stronger than the old which will break in their turn at the first test. This has been going on now for two years, and though in the course of things, it is inevitable that Samson will be beaten, one must admit that he has put up a game fight.

Combative Nixon squinting and pointing. *Star Collection*

July 7, 1974

This afternoon on my way to get the car washed, out of curiosity I drove by the Supreme Court to take in the scene. On
those grand alabaster steps, I supposed that there were about
forty people sitting or sleeping in sleeping bags, waiting for the
doors to open tomorrow to be admitted to the court for the
first arguments in *United States vs. Richard Nixon.* How suc-
cinctly that puts this whole prosecution! Imagine! The United
States versus Richard Nixon.

Later I went running on the Mall. I'm always in training,
it seems, but now I was remembering that Clemenceau kept
himself fit all his life and was an excellent equestrian, fencer,
and marksman. As I ran toward the Washington Monument,
the president's helicopter passed low across the expanse of the
Mall, descending onto the White House lawn. I wonder if he
was returning from Key Biscayne or some other hiding place.
Oh, unfortunate, unhappy man, behold your doom.

When I came back, I mingled with the crowd waiting across
from the Supreme Court. Its size had more than quadrupled.
For only a hundred seats that are available in the court, there are
already 184 names on the guard's list, according to a young guy
I collared. The list becomes official at midnight, he told me, and
to stay on the list one has to stay on the steps. He's hoping for
some "wastage" on the list, because he was number 143.

July 8, 1974

I continue my shuttle between the Ellsberg break-in trial and the Judiciary Committee proceedings. At the US Courthouse, Ehrlichman is testifying today. The court is packed, with no available seat in the courtroom, so I waited for a half hour for someone to leave, looking through the square peephole in the door, hearing nothing but seeing both the judge and the witness table.

Judge Gerhard Gesell is a Santa Claus of a man with perfectly white hair and a face that changes color and expression throughout the afternoon, depending on how bored or excited he is. He is not a man to be trifled with. The jury had just been empaneled, and before dismissing them into the care of the marshals, he instructed them sternly about their sequestering. They began to file out, and as they were leaving, the spectators rose and began chatting, oblivious to the fact that court was still in session. Suddenly, Gesell's huge booming voice reverberated through the wood-paneled room:

"THIS COURT IS STILL IN SESSION. GUESTS WILL RESPECT THE DECORUM OF THE COURT OR THEY WILL NOT BE INVITED BACK!"

It surprised me that the judge questioned witnesses more actively than I might have expected. When he did, he cocked his head only slightly toward the witness, never looking directly at him, and never when the witness was replying.

The purpose of this style seems to deny the witness dignity or credence. Today, Mrs. Ehrlichman is accompanied by a black lady, and they constantly whisper to one another.

To these eyes, Ehrlichman seems like a terrible witness. He's arrogant and quibbling. He constantly asks the prosecutor what he means by a particular word in a question, as if this whole matter is a problem of semantics. Once he quibbles about the "philosophical meaning of the word 'examine,'" as in "examine the files of Dr. Fielding." I cannot imagine that the jury will be impressed.

His defense is that he did indeed approve a covert operation "to examine the files of Ellsberg's psychiatrist," but he thought he was approving a legal conventional investigation. How could such files be examined, short of a break-in, he was asked, when the psychiatrist had refused a look at them by the FBI a month earlier? "The means [of examining them] was never discussed," he answered. I could feel the collective but silent groans in the audience at this, and Judge Gesell grimaced. He was asked if the initial on a Plumbers document was his initial. "It would appear to be," he answered.

"Would it be fair to describe you as the architect of the Plumbers?" the prosecutor asked. Ehrlichman denied it, occasioning the prosecutor to read testimony from a Senate Appropriations Committee hearing in which he admitted that he was the architect. The courtroom snickered. Later, Ehrlichman insisted that he was only a "conduit" for Egil Krogh to the president. "Routine matters" were to be reported to him, but Krogh always had the option to go directly to the president. Frequently, Ehrlichman had a loss of memory when it came to key telephone records or key documents. At one point, he asserted that he had trained himself to skim documents, picking out only the important paragraphs and dismissing the rest from his mind as "grist" or "surplusage."

"I did not want to pack around in my memory a lot of surplusage or extra baggage," he said. "I couldn't function if I did."

To believe him, you had to regard him as slipshod and incompetent, approving covert, illegal operations without asking what they meant. It reminded me of the slip Senator Daniel Inouye made last summer after cross-examining Ehrlichman in the Select Committee hearings. Thinking the mic had been turned off, the senator quipped to an aide, "What a liar!" Later, he protested that he'd been misheard. He really said, "What a lawyer!"

The day in court ended dramatically. The judge asked the defense team about a subpoena that had been issued to compel the appearance of the secretary of state.

"We feel he is very material to the case, Your Honor."

"Is he under subpoena?"

"Yes, sir. We'd like Dr. Kissinger to appear when it is convenient for him."

"When does he return from overseas?" the judge asked.

"Tomorrow."

"Well, we could have him testify on Wednesday," Gesell said. "See that the proper authorities in the White House are informed."

"I'll certainly inform the authorities, Your Honor, but I don't know if I have the muscle to get him here."

Gesell waved him aside. "He's to be here at 9:30 Wednesday morning," he said curtly, and with that he left the bench.

July 10, 1974

Surely this is the homestretch. The Supreme Court has heard the arguments in *United States vs. Richard Nixon*, and virtually every report predicts that the decision will go against the president, perhaps unanimously. And today begins what is bound to be a litany of shocks from the Judiciary Committee.

This morning the *Post* carries the headline TRANSCRIPT LINKS NIXON TO COVER-UP, regarding the release of the unexpurgated Judiciary Committee version of conversations of which we already have seen only edited text. The second paragraph of the story contains this quotation: "I don't give a shit what happens. I want all to stonewall. . . . Let them plead the Fifth Amendment . . . cover up or anything else, if it'll save it . . . save the plan. That's the whole point." There is direct and indirect evidence that the president was involved as early as March 13, 1973, the week before the "cancer on the presidency" talk with John Dean that has hereto been the focus.

Of course, no one is surprised, but this new evidence is hard and devastating. In my omnibus piece, I argued that it was a mistake to concentrate on conversations nine months after the cover-up was put into place. But that is only logic. People don't get convicted or impeached on logic, only hard evidence. Now it's clear that several direct criminal charges can be proven convincingly, any one of which is enough

29

for removal. As Lincoln said to his secretary of war, Edwin Stanton, after Appomattox: "Your knots don't slip."

Last week a number of press reports indicated that the committee is indeed considering an omnibus impeachment article. Hard evidence for indictable crime, adding criminal counts to the general count, certainly helps. Matters are proceeding satisfactorily.

I must say I have the greatest respect for the way the Judiciary Committee conducted itself initially. Keeping their deliberations secret at first was wise. I accept the explanation that secrecy sped up the inquiry, protected the rights of the accused, and educated the members at a deliberate pace beyond the glare of television cameras. Now we can inspect the fruits of their labors.

The language of the taped conversations is low, banal, and mean, indicating an absence of thought or certainly any high purpose. Nixon doesn't even know how to swear right. Who ever heard of anyone saying, "It's a son-of-a-bitching hard thing."

How different from the language in the Supreme Court on Monday.

"Now enmeshed in almost five hundred pages of briefs," said Jaworski, "when boiled down, this case presents a fundamental issue: who is the arbiter of what the Constitution says? . . . Now the president may be right in how he reads the Constitution. But he may also be wrong. And if he is wrong, who is there to tell him so? And if there is no one, then the president, of course, is free to pursue his course of erroneous interpretations. What then becomes of our constitutional form of government?"

And St. Clair, who this morning's *Post* praises for the brilliance, if illogic, of his Supreme Court performance, constantly refers to his adversary as his "brother," and then turns around and casts doubt on whether the president will obey the Supreme Court ruling.

"Are you still leaving it up to this Court to decide this case?" Judge Thurgood Marshall asked.

"Yes, in a sense," St. Clair replied.

"In what sense?"

"In the sense that this court has the obligation to determine the law. The president has the obligation to carry out his constitutional duties."

It was Philip Roth who spawned the joke nearly a year ago about what the president would say after he was impeached and convicted. "Just as the House and Senate have their responsibilities, I have mine, and I will stay in office."

Street theater. *Star Collection*

July 12, 1974

Last night we had dinner with the Udalls, and, as always, it was a fine evening. Morris has launched his presidential candidacy, but he does not seem to take himself too seriously. He was fascinating about the White House strategy. It is this: to narrow the focus of the inquiry to the smallest detail (March 21); at the same time broadening the president's rights as much as possible (St. Clair's ability to question committee witnesses); and most importantly, making everyone in Congress feel guilty about expressing any opinion on the evidence, since they are potential grand jurors.

"If the public gets the idea that the case is circumstantial, impeachment is dead," Morris said. "Circumstantial means something other than substantial."

Thank goodness, the evening was not all impeachment talk. It afforded another example of why I've always had an attitude akin to hero worship toward my old boss, Stewart, ever since he hired me as a twenty-three-year-old researcher as a so-called confidential assistant, when he was the youngest member of John F. Kennedy's Cabinet and allowed me to work with him on his seminal conservation classic *The Quiet Crisis*. In true Camelot fashion, he read poems of Archibald MacLeish. And I got to spend an emotional ten minutes with their troubled, poignant son, Scott, who is back from Canada, where he was an Army deserter, and free now of obligations to the military after his dishonorable discharge. In dispensing his punishment, the colonel who was his judge said, "You are a disgrace to your family."

Still unsettled and very vulnerable, Scott was very cautious. We talked only in pleasantries. Beforehand, Lee Udall told me, "he's afraid you might ask him a lot of heavy questions." The encounter conjured up my anger once again about the absence of any action on amnesty for the fifty thousand refugees abroad from the Vietnam War. My fury over the additional twenty thousand pointless combat deaths in Vietnam during the Nixon years is still great and definitely colors my attitude toward this president.

Here are a few more anecdotes from the past few days that I should record. Two days ago, I persuaded my father to come down from his high perch in the *New York Times* and attend the Ehrlichman trial. He did so, and, as usual, the courtroom was jammed. So the esteemed columnist entered anyway and stood at the back of the room by the marshal to watch, even though, I suppose, he knew full well this was against the rules. He noticed that his good friend, Judge Gary Gesell, motioned to his secretary from the bench and whispered something to her, motioning in Dad's direction. Good, Dad thought, my friend Gary is going to do something special for me, like finding me a front-row seat. He did do something. He had Dad thrown out of the courtroom! That night on the phone, chagrined but also amused, Dad said, "He wanted to show me who was in charge."

Today the Judiciary Committee released its first batch of evidence, nearly five thousand pages of unexpurgated material. On television James St. Clair is doing his best to spin the reaction. There were no surprises in these pages, he said. It amounts only to a circumstantial case against the president.

Later in the day, I took a cab over to the courthouse, expecting another ordinary day of point/counterpoint. But, shockingly, the place was cordoned off by what seemed like a hundred policeman in riot gear. I could only think that Ehrlichman had done something crazy. But no. Two desperate black inmates have seized seven hostages and are holding them in a cellblock in the basement of the courthouse. I hadn't seen that many police gathered in one place since my wife and I were gassed on Dupont Circle in 1969 during a Vietnam protest.

July 13, 1974

Ehrlichman is guilty! Convicted of conspiracy, lying, and perjury. The trial is over, and this will not help his boss. St. Clair, having argued to the Supreme Court that the tapes are inextricably intertwined with the impeachment process, now says, "The impeachment of the president is separate and distinct from the criminal prosecution of Mr. Ehrlichman."

Judge Gesell's instructions to the jury seem to have been crucial. Once at trial, he had snapped at Ehrlichman's defense lawyer, "This is not a semantic case," referring to the lawyer's consistent use of the term "covert operation" instead of "burglary." The judge cautioned that nothing short of a duly authorized search warrant could have justified entry into Fielding's office. "An individual cannot escape criminal liability," Gesell told the jury, "simply because he sincerely but incorrectly believes that his acts are justified in the name of patriotism or national security, or a need to create an unfavorable press image, or that his superiors have the authority without a warrant to suspend the constitutional protections of the Fourth Amendment."

And then this beautiful statement: "There is no evidence that the president authorized such a search. But as a matter of law neither he nor any official or any agency such as the FBI or the CIA has the authority to order it." So enough of this business about the president being above the law. Ehrlichman becomes the highest official so far to be convicted. Only the chief of staff, Haldeman, remains. Ehrlichman has not given up, however. He intends to appeal, he says, because of his "inability to get a fair trial in this district."

Nineteen Convictions Minus One. *National Portrait Gallery © 1973 by Philip Lief and Marcel Feigel*

July 15, 1974

Lunch today with ACLU's legal director, Chuck Morgan, and Jack Nelson of the *Los Angeles Times*. The conversation devolved to the question of whether the country is really tired of the whole business. Nelson thinks so. Morgan feels only the newsmen are tired of the story. Nelson has been covering the story for two years and would like a break.

"I'd like to go cover conservation in the Okefenokee Swamp," he said.

No wonder reporters are frustrated. The confidentiality of the Judiciary Committee has been humiliating for newsmen. Take this item on the news tonight. Colson testified in executive session before the committee. Outside the committee room, one congressman said Colson implicated the president in ordering the Ellsberg break-in. Another member, Charles Wiggins of California, who is the president's articulate defender, says he heard no such thing. What are we to believe? The confusion inspires contempt for the process, and this, of course, redounds to the president's favor.

Meanwhile, the street theater for impeachment flourishes.

July 18, 1974

Tonight, just for fun, I attended the banquet of the National Citizens' Committee for Fairness to the Presidency in the massive banquet hall of the Shoreham Hotel. Lionel Hampton, "the president's favorite musician," kicked things off by having the audience sing with him:

> "We need Nixon
> Let's stay with Nixon.
> Let's help him finish the job
> People know him.
> So let's all show him
> We're sure he's the best man for the job."

A Baptist minister from Rocky Mount, North Carolina, Reverend Ross Moyer, delivered the invocation with a plea for "divine light and guidance for our beloved president" and for divine vengeance for the "malicious press." The founder of the group, Rabbi Baruch Korff, then took over and introduced the honored guests at the head table, "my conservative ideologue, Patrick Buchanan"; the ambassador from Tunisia, "representing another great president, Habib Bourgiba"; Senator Carl Curtis of Nebraska, "a man I'd like to adulate"; Secretaries of Commerce and Agriculture, Frederick Dent and Earl Butz; Leonard Garment, the president's lawyer; Reverend

John McLaughlin, "a Jewish Jesuit"; and finally, the Romanian ambassador, representing a "president who is quite independent," Nicolae Ceaușescu.

The rabbi then picked up on Reverend Moyer's theme about the press. In a marvelous gravelly voice, he charged that the Fourth Estate was holding the other three estates captive. "They have an investment in impeachment," he said. "These giants of the media are the prosecutors. They're like the Red Queen of *Alice in Wonderland*. When the people cried, 'Let us hear the evidence and then we will sentence, the Red Queen replied, 'No, let us sentence first and then hear the evidence.'"

My dinner partner was a handsome, elderly lady from Manhattan named Miss Autumn Sims, who said she had gotten up at 4:00 a.m. this morning to get down here for the banquet. "I don't like to be rushed," she allowed. She assured me that this was really a grassroots group that truly represented America. "Of course, there are not many grassroots people in New York City. Well, there are, but they're ethnic peoples. I have nothing against that. There are many very nice people with that background. But they don't like Nixon. I don't know why exactly. I suppose it's because they're suspicious of anyone who is grassroots America."

When a black minister, Dr. Herbert Hinkle from the Cathedral of Faith in Inkster, Michigan, took the podium, Miss Sims whispered to me that she liked "to see a black man up there. It gives them dignity and confidence." After a bit of gospel singing from his choir, Dr. Hinkle's voice filled the great room. "Without a song, this road will never end. It is not well known that black people are concerned about fairness to the president," and he called upon Solomon, Amos, and Jesus. And finally, without explaining the point, he quoted Booker

T. Washington's famous line, "In all things social we can be as separate as the fingers yet one as the hand in all things essential to mutual progress." I thought the thrust of the line had been Washington's justification for segregation.

Then the president called in by phone. Korff read to him from the program: "Mr. President, those who have admired you since your political youth can now only paraphrase Robert Frost: We do not find you changed from him we know, only more sure of all you thought was true. Despite your detractors, history is shaped by the stalwart and vindicates the brave. In your case, Mr. President, history's verdict is already clear. And now, sir, we are ready to hear from you."

The usual banalities followed: the greatness of America depending upon people in great enterprises, greater than themselves . . . rally behind the office of the presidency . . . others will follow in this great office "beginning in January 1977 (much applause) . . . quoting Lincoln about the "last best hope," and finally, "I will not let you down." When it was over, Korff held up the telephone receiver. The crowd cheered and went into a "WE WANT NIXON" chant. "We love you deeply," Korff said, and rang off.

Other program speakers followed. Secretary Butz, ever the wit, told the audience that if Nixon had walked on the waters of the Red Sea, the AP would report: Nixon walks on the Red Sea, and the UP would report: Nixon walks on the Red Sea, and the *Washington Post* would report: Nixon can't swim. That got a big laugh. Senator Curtis, dressed in a white linen suit and big red bow tie, called Nixon the "greatest peacemaker in the history of the world." And Korff ended the evening with the plans for the rest of the week. Tomorrow morning, the group would have their "Genesis" at the Shoreham, their "Exodus" to the Capitol, going with the "zeal of Leviticus" where they would write their own "Deuteronomy."

I said good-bye to Miss Sims and filed out of the room past the table displaying Korff's book for the reasonable price of $1.30. Leafing through its pages to the interview with Nixon, my eyes fell on the important passages. The Ehrlichman verdict was a "blot on justice." If I were a "liberal, Watergate would be a blip." Comparing Watergate to Teapot Dome is like comparing "applies with oranges and rather poor oranges at that. And finally, Watergate is the broadest and thinnest scandal in American history, because, what is it about?"

As I finish this entry the morning, the *New York Times* editorial responded to his question with a question of its own.

"Is it possible that at this late date, he still really doesn't know?"

July 19, 1974

The Judiciary Committee concluded its hearings two days ago, and the televised debate is set to begin five days from now. Today the tension in the committee room is higher than it has been since I've been here. John Doar, the chief Democratic counsel, is addressing himself to "theories of impeachment," and it's clear that he's changed into an impassioned advocate. The switch was something to watch, because till now there's been a good deal of talk about how dull his presentations of the evidence are. The languor of his style is a partial reason why the Committee decided against open hearings at the outset. Doar evidently used to play portions of the presidential tapes as a reward to congressmen for paying attention.

I stood in the hallway outside the committee room, chatting with my friend Paul Houston of the *Los Angeles Times*. The atmosphere is suddenly altogether different, he said. The proceeding has always ebbed and flowed. In fact, he was preparing a story about impeachment doldrums. Now that idea is tabled. The mood has suddenly received a jolt of electricity. Paul thinks that the Committee's release of the evidence in such massive doses over the past week has been brilliant public relations, The president's defenders, like Congressman Wiggins, who are thought to be "persuadable," are coming under increasing pressure.

Later in the day, I talked with Phil Geyelin, the *Post's* editorial chief (we're talking about another op-ed). He had spoken with former Supreme Court Justice Arthur Goldberg earlier, and Goldberg feels that the impeachment staff has undermined its case with too much evidence and delay, but Geyelin disagrees. Not only impeachment, but conviction is now very likely, he thinks. Perhaps . . . and perhaps not.

About 12:30 p.m., Republican congressman William Cohen of Maine came rushing out of the committee room and dashed through the press without comment. Usually, he tarries and talks openly and cordially. His vote will be crucial. If he votes for impeachment, it's likely he will be the Republican floor manager in the House. The poor reporters were forced to jog alongside down the hall.

Less bashful members went before the cameras. Republican Charles Sandman of New Jersey said that Doar had presented five sets of possible impeachment articles. He was opposed to an omnibus article, which was then under consideration. But Lawrence Hogan (Republican from Maryland), who is thought to be one of the "persuadables," said he had no problem with the consideration of a general impeachment article, covering the entire mosaic of misdeeds, so long as it followed specific charges. Another New Jersey Republican, Joseph Maraziti, also drew a crowd. He wished Doar had been more specific in the allegations against the president, and he would wait until Monday to hear the arguments of the minority counsel. After listening to testimony for ten weeks, hadn't he drawn any conclusions? I asked him. When he said no, the Korff people who were hovering around the fringe of the press applauded. When the scrum broke up and people began to drift away, one of Korff's people said:

"Something stinks around here. It must be the press."

Tonight, in the evening paper, the *Washington Star-News*, Rabbi Korff has a full-page ad. The text reads that the country is approaching a "Constitutional Armageddon, a showdown between our traditional form of government and leftist-radical mobbery." Who is John Doar working for? the ad asks: "for those who weep for the Viet Cong victory of which the President has cheated them?" And then:

"How many Democrats of the Judiciary Committee will recognize John Doar for the paid assassin he is?"

John Doar and his detractors. *Star Collection*

July 23, 1974

A satisfying afternoon. I went to the House for credentials to attend the televised Judiciary debate, which begins tomorrow. Outside the House chambers, I sent a page in to ask Representative Bill Steiger, Republican of Wisconsin, to come out. (He was my older brother's roommate at the University of Wisconsin and a very thoughtful guy.) In a fifteen-minute chat, he complained that the press was not giving enough attention to the individual conscience of each congressman. "They're always looking for a political or self-serving motive from a politician."

The pack then scrambled to the press conference of Lawrence Hogan (Republican from Maryland). It was as if Bill Steiger had intuited the importance. Hogan began discursively. Impeachment is a "quasi-criminal procedure that requires the highest standard of proof, proof beyond a reasonable doubt.

"After having read and reread, sifted and tested the mass of information which came before us, I have come to the conclusion that Richard M. Nixon has, beyond a reasonable doubt, committed impeachable offenses, which, in my judgment, are of sufficient magnitude that he should be removed from office. The president has lied repeatedly, deceiving public officials and the American people. He has withheld information necessary for our system of justice to work. Instead of cooperating with prosecutors and investigators, he concealed and covered up evidence and coached witnesses, so that their testimony would show things that were not true. He approved the payment of what he knew to be blackmail to buy silence of an important Watergate witness. He praised and rewarded those who he knew had committed perjury. He participated in a conspiracy to obstruct justice."

I stood aghast. Was I really watching this? I had goose bumps. He went on:

"Clearly, this is an occasion when party loyalty demands too much. To base this decision on politics would not only violate my own conscience, but would be a breach of my oath of office to uphold the Constitution. Those who oppose impeachment say it would weaken the presidency. In my view, if we do not impeach this president after all that he has done, we would be weakening the presidency even more."

So he is the first Republican. How many more will there be? In questioning after his statement, Hogan predicted that at least five and possibly eight of the seventeen members of the committee would vote yea. Inevitably, the cynics among the reporters were speculating about ulterior motives. Wasn't Hogan running for governor of Maryland? The *Baltimore Sun* reporter crafted his gotcha: Is Hogan deserting a sinking ship? This implies, of course, that Hogan is a rat.

At home tonight in my cozy turret, Sam Ervin's last literary reference in his final letter to his committee last year occurred to me. It was the poem of nineteenth-century poet Josiah Gilbert Holland called "The Day's Demand," but Ervin said he liked to think of it as "America's Prayer."

> GOD, give us men! A time like this demands
> Strong minds, great hearts, true faith and ready hands;
> Men whom the lust of office does not kill;

Men whom the spoils of office can not buy;
Men who possess opinions and a will;
Men who have honor; men who will not lie;
Men who can stand before a demagogue
And damn his treacherous flatteries without winking!
Tall men, sun-crowned, who live above the fog
In public duty, and in private thinking;
For while the rabble, with their thumb-worn creeds,
Their large professions and their little deeds,
Mingle in selfish strife, lo! Freedom weeps,
Wrong rules the land and waiting Justice sleeps.

July 26, 1974

I haven't entered anything in this diary in the past few days, and it is because I'm overwhelmed by what has happened. Two days ago, the Supreme Court ruled 8–0 that the president must turn over sixty-four tape recordings to the special prosecutor. I was there. Later that evening, the debate on articles of impeachment began in the Judiciary Committee. I watched it, as if it was a night baseball game, at Chuck Morgan's house on Constitution Avenue over fried chicken and beer. Yesterday, each member had fifteen minutes to speak, and I attended the morning session. Today, with the statements of all members completed, the debate moves to consideration of articles of impeachment.

The papers are full of stories about the dwindling support of the president. On television this morning, congressmen are predicting that seven of the seventeen Republicans on the committee will vote for one or more articles, making the vote 28–10. Half my mind is on the debate as I sit here in my little study with the television on without sound. But I must put down my memories of the past few days before it's too late. Events are rushing so fast!

On Wednesday I was admitted late to the corridor on the side of the Supreme Court chambers reserved for the press, getting one of the last admission tickets. Authors must take a back seat to the working press, and that's as it should be.

Supporters of both sides mingled outside the courtroom ready to receive their victor after the decision was rendered. Once inside, I watched the decision on tiptoes from the back of the chamber, past heads of well-groomed hair, through a brass grate, and around a post. With all the wrangling for a clear beam, I could see only about half the bench. But what a set! The backdrop of the lovely rich red damask curtain imparts a stateliness. I could see the ceiling best of all: luscious red and blue background for the plaster, flower-like designs. The room is magnificent—what I could see of it. There is something Roman about the scene.

One could feel the excitement of the audience, as there was no certainty how the Court will rule on *United States vs. Richard Nixon*. But the presence of the special prosecutor at the counsel's table gave a hint.

The Chief Justice, Warren Burger, a Republican and a Minnesotan appointed by Nixon five years ago, began with a lengthy, convoluted discourse on the jurisdiction of the Court and the law governing subpoenas, Rule 17(c) of the Federal Rules of Criminal Procedure, before he addressed the central question. The legalisms, dense as they were, added to the drama. When he finally got to the claim of privilege by the president, the tension was high. I admit I had trouble in following the thicket of his verbiage.

> Neither the doctrine of separation of powers, nor the need for confidentiality of high-level communications, can sustain an absolute unqualified Presidential privilege of immunity from the judicial process under all circumstances. . . . When privilege depends solely on the broad, undifferentiated claim of public interest in

the confidentiality of such conversations, a confrontation of other values arises. Absent a claim of need to protect military, diplomatic, or sensitive national security secrets, we find it difficult to accept the argument that even the very important interest of confidentiality of Presidential communications is significantly diminished by the production of such material in *in-camera* inspection with all the protection that a District Court will be obliged to provide.

Burger is no tower of lucidity, his opinions notorious for being turgid, making it arduous for the public to parse their meaning. He needs a good editor, but I understood the gist. In short, the presidential privilege of confidentiality is not absolute. It has to be balanced against the overriding dictates of criminal law. In balancing the two competing principles, a president will almost always lose, especially since grand jury deliberations are secret.

Burger concluded: "In this case we must weigh the importance of the general privilege of confidentiality of Presidential communications in performance of his responsibilities against the inroads of such privilege of the fair administration of criminal justice. . . . The generalized assertion of privilege must yield to the demonstrated, specific need for evidence in a pending criminal trial."

Then most of all, I understood: "Affirmed." Unanimous 8–0. What, I wondered, would have been the implications of a narrow loss like 5–3? Would it have encouraged Nixon to resist the decision?

In the hallway afterward, I joined the cluster of people around Jaworski as he answered questions. The answer I remember best is, "I could not be more pleased if I had written the decision myself." It was, he said, as historic a decision as the Supreme Court has ever made. After the reporters' questions dwindled, he tarried in the hallway, leaning against a column, signing autographs on visitors' entry cards like a Broadway star, patiently enjoying it. I had imagined a short man like Rodino, who is only five three, but Jaworski is tall, well over six feet, and speaks in dignified Texas tones.

He then strode out onto the steps, where a throng of about five hundred people greeted him with cheers and shouts of congratulation. The scene was astonishing. Here was the prosecutor of the president of the United States receiving ecstatic jubilation from a crowd of ordinary Americans. What a time this is!

Later in the afternoon came the flash that the president would have a statement at 7:00 p.m. Will he resign? What could be a better time? He could say, "I will not be the president to breach the confidentiality of the Oval Office" and depart on a technical issue. Would he ever have another chance to leave on a more-or-less dignified note? Surely not after the Judiciary Committee recommends impeachment, if it does, or if the full House votes for it, if it will, since that would be an admission of guilt.

At 7:00 p.m., James St. Clair simply announced that the president would comply fully with the Court's decision. It was a bland, straightforward announcement, something of an anticlimax after so much presidential brinksmanship as to whether he would obey a "definitive" decision. (I think again of Philip Roth's joke.) How exemplary of Washington's culture of obfuscation is Nixon's pale response to the decision later. "I am gratified to note that the Court reaffirmed both the validity and the importance of the principle of executive privilege, the principle I had sought to maintain."

The important point is that the decision was not only definitive but unanimous. Together with Hogan's defection and the Republican colleagues who will probably follow him, we're entering the final act of the king's dethroning. The king? The potentate? The imperial president? I like best the language of Senator Charles Sumner of Massachusetts during the impeachment trial of Andrew Johnson:

"He once declared himself to be the Moses of the colored people. Behold him now, the Pharaoh. With such treachery in such a cause there can be no parley. . . . Pharaoh is at the bar of the Senate for judgment."

Special Prosecutor Leon Jaworski. *Library of Congress, Prints & Photographs*

July 27, 1974

And so on to the debate. This will be its third day, and some think its last. Near midnight last night the first symbolic vote was taken in the Judiciary Committee on a motion to strike the first article against the president: "making false or misleading statements to lawfully authorized investigative officers and employees of the United States." It lost 27 to 11 and thus will stand as Article One. I expect that, as in the Senate vote in the Andrew Johnson case, once the first vote is taken and passes, the others will follow quickly in succession with the same result.

I spent the day in the committee room. The room itself is awesome, with its towering ceiling and fine wood paneling and massive seal of the United States on the wall facing the thirty-eight members of the committee, the grand jurors. The floor space, by contrast, is rather small, and there are only fourteen seats for the public. The rest is reserved for the press and staff.

The opening statements of the congressmen were impressive, a fine display of public oratory, as fine as I have ever witnessed. The anguish of the Republican members is palpable and poignant, as many try to rise above a strict partisan view. Some members stuck to the evidence in their speeches, and their grasp of it now is astonishing.

I'm struck again at the wisdom of keeping the early hearings secret. The stage of floundering about for understanding was kept from public view. When these proceedings became open and public, the customary shallowness and flippancy was absent. Members came off not only as deep experts, but as historians and legal scholars and even moral philosophers as well, all very aware of the historic import of their task. They were exhibiting Carlyle's first test of heroism: sincerity.

As usual, I'm drawn to the occasional literary allusions that are presented. Lawrence Hogan of Maryland, for example, was full of mixed metaphors. He asserted that many Republicans were looking for an "arrow to the heart," but there was none. The evidence was like a "virus that creeps up on you slowly and gradually, until its obviousness is overwhelming." Searching for one document or sentence that would do the president in, he said, was like looking at "a mosaic and focusing in on one single tile and saying, I see nothing wrong with that one little piece."

Conspiracies were not born in sunlight, said William Cohen of Maine. "They are hatched in dark recesses, amid whispers and code words and verbal signals. The footprints of guilt must often be traced with the searchlight of probability." It was he who took on Morris Udall's point about circumstantial evidence. Circumstantial evidence, he said, is just as valid as direct evidence; in fact, sometimes it is even stronger evidence. "If you went to sleep at night and the ground was bare, and you woke up with fresh snow on the ground, then certainly you would conclude as a reasonable person that snow had fallen, even though you had not seen it." John Seiberling of Ohio improved upon the metaphor. "Some circumstantial evidence is very strong, as when you find a trout in the milk."

The pro-impeachment forces do not have a monopoly on allusions to sunlight. The defenders of the president were not be outdone on this semantic turf. David Dennis of Indiana, one of the president's staunchest defenders, insisted that someone had to present the case "in the cold light of the judicial day," and unless there was a legally provable case, the committee ought not to proceed. "Hearsay will not do. Inference upon inference will not do. Prior recorded testimony and other legal proceedings to which the president was *not* a party will not serve."

For me, Barbara Jordan of Texas was the most moving. During the past days she has gone twice to the National Archives to read the Constitution in the original. "Today I am an inquisitor," she began. "My faith in the Constitution is whole. It is complete. It is total. I am not going to sit here and be an idle spectator to the diminution, the subversion, the destruction of the Constitution." And then she quoted the Federalist Papers, No. 65. "Who can so properly be the inquisitors for the nation as the representatives of the nation themselves."

As one commentator is saying in the paper this morning, the members finally came down from Olympus. The wrangling began. The interchanges were sharp and often partisan, and at first, focused on narrow and technical issues over the specific wording of the articles. But at last my advocacy for an omnibus article to encompass them all was addressed, though in a different way. The first two articles, obstruction of justice in the cover-up and abuse of power, combine the general with the specific, and so that seems like the best of both worlds. Article One states that the president "made it his policy" to obstruct justice. That violated his oath of office and his duty faithfully to execute the laws. Then it goes on to nine specific points of obstruction.

Should these nine charges be cited chapter and verse, to enable the defendant to understand precisely what he is being charged with? Did not the president have the same rights as a common criminal? asked Sandman of New Jersey. And Wiggins of California keeps insisting that the proposers of Article One should specify when this policy was declared.

At last, five hours into the proceeding, William Hungate, Democrat from Missouri, gave the proceeding a moment of much-needed humor. About the possibility that the president would not understand the general charges against him, Hungate said, "If they don't understand what we're talking about now, they don't know a hawk from a handsaw." And on the charge that the proposers were piling inference upon inference, he said,

"If a guy brought an elephant through that door, and one of us said, that is an elephant, some of the doubters would say, you know, that is an inference. It could be a mouse with a glandular condition."

Nixon as a piñata. *Star Collection*

July 29, 1974

This morning the committee room was cleared. There was a bomb threat. Rumor was that a plane had left National Airport and the pilot intended to crash it into the Rayburn Building. As the audience quickly left the room, Rodino and Doar sat talking quietly for a few minutes, with Rodino often glancing out of the window up at the sky. Then the chairman quickly left, and people reported that he was weeping.

Two days ago, the committee moved forward to vote on Article One. We hear the phrase "much has been made" frequently. Much has been made of the historic nature of the vote. Much has been made about how the vote brought no joy to any of the grand jurors, pro and con. Congressman Walter Flowers of Alabama, an important swing vote, called this an "unhappy day," when members had to vote on "this terrible proposition." He had nothing to gain personally or politically from it. "But I know what I must do."

Through most of the afternoon the press seats were sparsely occupied, but at 6:30 p.m. they filled rapidly. The anticipation was thick, even if there was no doubt of the outcome. As the clerk called the roll, it seemed as if a contest was afoot for the longest face. But these long faces worry me. I was watching for compassion, but not sympathy.

Yet I have to remind myself that this is only the first step, the Judiciary Committee as grand jury. Nixon can drag this thing out and fight to the bitter end. Earlier in the day, a White House aide speculates that a Senate trial could last nine to eleven months. Time passes slowly.

As I write this on this Saturday night, I turn on the television to a baseball game: Indians and Tigers. Curt Gowdy announces that a vote on the Second Article is imminent. "We'll keep you posted," he says. Meanwhile, the count on the batter is 2 and 2.

As I toggle between the game and the debate, William Hungate, the wit from Missouri, is saying, "Yes, Virginia, there is a law of agency." They're debating about Nixon as the "principal" to be held accountable for the acts of his "agents," specifically for the misuse of the IRS, the FBI, the CIA, and the Justice Department in the cover-up. Generally, that Nixon did not "take care that the laws be faithfully executed." So the Second Article rests as much on what the president did not do as what he did do. It is the crime of nonfeasance or negligence.

The Second Article, about abuse of power, reads: "In all of this Richard M. Nixon has acted in a manner contrary to his trust as President and subversive of constitutional government, to the great prejudice of the cause of law and justice, and to the manifest injury of the people of the United States. Wheretofore, Richard M. Nixon, by such conduct, warrants impeachment and trial and removal from office."

Beneficently, the committee takes a break for dinner, and I walk over to my favorite little Greek restaurant on Pennsylvania Avenue, taking along Clemenceau's diary. Halfway through a beer and reading an entry from September 10, 1867, I look up to see George Danielson (Democrat from California), a delightful character with a twinkle in his eye and hair parted just above his ear, and James Mann (Democrat from South

Carolina), the chief drafter of impeachment articles, take a seat next to my table. Danielson bumped into me as he sat down in the cramped space and apologized. On a whim, I told him I was reading something that might interest him, and showed him the entry:

"The war between the President and Congress goes on, complicated from time to time by some unexpected turn. Contrary to all that has happened, is happening, and will happen, the legislative power has the upper hand. Congress may, when it pleases, take the President by the ear and lead him down from his high seat, and he can do nothing about it except to struggle and shout."

Danielson read the passage quickly and handed it back to me. "There's some truth to that," he said, disinterested. He thinks I'm a nut.

Late in the evening, the Second Article passes 28 to 10.

Congresswoman Barbara Jordan of Texas announces her
vote for impeachment. *Courtesy US House of Representatives
Photography Office*

July 30, 1974

Against Article Three, the president's failure to honor committee subpoenas, the most eloquent and effective of the president's defenders, Charles Wiggins of California, makes this argument. In voting for the first two articles, the committee had determined that there was enough evidence to impeach the president. But now, with this Third Article, the committee asserts that the president has withheld evidence and defied congressional subpoenas for specific information so the committee cannot perform its duty for lack of evidence. This is a contradiction, says Wiggins. Either there is enough evidence, and you impeach him for what you have. Or there is not enough evidence because the president has not provided it, and you impeach him for that. You can't have it both ways. Tom Railsback (Republican from Illinois) weighs in a bit less eloquently, calling the Third Article "political overkill."

In disputing this position for the majority, Seiberling of Ohio evoked the famous quote of Sir Edward Coke in the so-called Case of Prohibitions in 1610. "The king cannot be judge of his own cause." Coke's commentaries had a deep influence on the American Founding Fathers in their crafting the concept for the American presidency, and this principle became enshrined in constitutional law. Executive power was not to be absolute and unrestricted. I looked up the actual

Coke reference. King James I had argued that the king has absolute power in his royal person to decide cases of law, and the judges were merely his delegates. Coke demurred. "The King in his own person cannot adjudge any case, either criminal—as treason, felony etc. . . . but this ought to be determined and decided in some court of justice, according to the Law and Custom of England."

The Third Article passed 21 to 17.

How quickly the impeachment of the president has become commonplace! Tension has evaporated. Long faces are gone, along with sober statements about the gravity of the process. Some members even smile when they vote, a reflection of the fact that the public now views the proceedings favorably.

If the members generally comport themselves with dignity and learnedness, occasionally there is still nastiness. Sandman of New Jersey charged last night that the debate over the president's tax evasions was arranged by the majority to appear on prime-time television. The curmudgeonly Jack Brooks of Texas said the charge reminded him of a mother who gave her son two ties. When the boy came down the next morning wearing one of them, the mother burst out tearfully that her son did not like the other tie. Hogan of Maryland was asked querulously how much more of these proceedings the American public could stand. He replied that the members were not engaged in entertaining the public. This was serious business, and they must proceed with great care and deliberation.

Today there's a report that after three weeks in San Clemente, the president spent his first day back in the White House listening alone in the Lincoln Room to the tapes he must now turn over to Judge Sirica after the Supreme Court decision. It reminds me of the line from Clemenceau's diary, just before Andrew Johnson departs the White House.

"Mr. Johnson, like Medea, stands absolutely alone. He is his sole remaining friend. Unhappily, he does not suffice."

August 1, 1974

A compulsion drew me to the Ehrlichman sentencing yesterday morning. Tension was high as Judge Gesell entered the court to the booming voice of the bailiff. "God Save the United States and this Honorable Court!" The judge's first words were a warning. No one would be permitted to enter or leave the courtroom until the judgment was proclaimed. The judge asked the defendant if he had anything to say. In soft tones, Ehrlichman replied that of all the people in the room, only he knew for sure whether he was guilty or innocent of the charges, and he was innocent.

Very well, after this ritual of allowing the prisoner in the dock his last words, the judge proceeded with the business at hand. "This shameful incident in our history," began his pronouncement. The Constitution had been ignored. A federal prosecution was dismissed. Deceit and falsehoods were pervasive throughout. That Ehrlichman had held the highest position of public trust made his crime worse, and the jury was convinced that these dastardly deeds had been done with Ehrlichman's consent. The gavel came down: twenty months to five years.

When it came to him, Liddy was true to form. When Judge Gesell asked him if he had anything to say, the good soldier said, "Nothing at all." Gesell called his crime "clear and deliberate" and sentenced him to one to three years.

On to Barker and Martinez. In his plea to the judge, their defense lawyer, Daniel Schultz, evoked Thoreau: "If a man does not keep pace with his companions, perhaps it is because he hears a different drum. Let him step to the music that he hears, however measured or far away." Barker and Martinez purportedly listened to a Cuban drum, different from the rest of us and quite far away. For his final words to the court, Martinez plead in his heavy accent, "My intention in this matter was never to be a criminal or a thug, Your Honor." Surprisingly, Schultz's argument and Martinez's words seemed to persuade Gesell. Saying the two had suffered enough, Gesell gave them three years' probation.

Outside the courthouse Ehrlichman continued to whine that every day public officials have to balance the rights of individuals against the larger good of the country. He likened the Ellsberg break-in to the farmer who gives up his land for an air base, or the young man who gives several years of his life to military service.

As a veteran who had given three years of my life to military service during the Vietnam era, when twenty thousand more soldiers had lost their lives during Ehrlichman's watch, this appalling assertion made my blood boil.

August 2, 1974

Yesterday I went to see Congressman Paul McCloskey (Republican from California) to talk about immunity for the president. On a quick count, I figure that Nixon is subject to indictment under at least fifteen federal criminal statutes, not including the tax evasions. Last year I. F. Stone wrote that the president's defense in Watergate all along could be viewed as a strategy to stay out of jail.

Earlier in the year, McCloskey and Wilbur Mills, the powerful Democrat from Arkansas (an unlikely duo) proposed immunity in return for resignation. It was a straight political trade-off then. But now I wanted to propose to McCloskey that immunity for Nixon be tied to amnesty for all Vietnam war resisters. It would be a Reconciliation Act to bind Vietnam *and* Watergate together and finally put them both behind us. McCloskey seemed intrigued by the idea, and we wondered together how it might best be done, through an act of Congress or somehow appealing to the new president to use his pardoning power for the previous disgraced president.

As we were talking, McCloskey broke to take a phone call, and when he hung up, he said, "The nut is tightening." We drifted back to the subject of pardons. The joke around the Capitol is that as the Senate roll was called in his Senate trial, somewhere around the *H*s (Roman Hruska, Republican from

Nebraska) perhaps, Nixon would start signing twenty-two pardons for all twenty-two of his cronies.

"His pardoning power is absolute until the convicting vote is cast," he said.

As a politician, McCloskey views the immunity question two ways: publicity and action. He could make a splash with a public proposal of his own, but he was more interested in making such a proposal work in Congress. He thought out loud about trying to put together a coalition of liberals (Edward Kennedy, Charles Percy, and others) to support an immunity package. I'm to call him back on Monday. Meanwhile, I'll write a piece for *Newsweek* proposing this.

This morning, meanwhile, I talked to an aide to Wilbur Mills. The congressman's reasoning is still the same, he said. Immunity could be traded for resignation. But the timing was like a quick opening play in football: such a bill could only pass after the House had voted for impeachment, but before the beginning of the Senate trial. There is no chance after conviction.

Later in the day Frank Mankiewicz and I went to see Senator Weicker (Republican of Connecticut). He is quite a high-power character but rather one-dimensional. We had hoped to get him in a philosophical mood about the Select Committee deliberations last summer where he was such a star. He seemed quite content to speak of himself as an important figure of history: his relationship with the CIA director, Patrick Gray, and John Dean, his investigation of the Internal Security Division of the Justice Department, his relationship to the Cubans. In a column somewhere today, he's mentioned as a potential vice president for the next president.

Though he was such a prominent figure in the hearings last summer, his star seemed to fade at the end. His rhetoric is harsh, angry, and often pious, good at the beginning, but grating later. It is the Southerners like folksy Sam Ervin in the Select Committee hearings and gentlemanly M. Caldwell Butler of Virginia in the Judiciary Committee who are the most interesting and three-dimensional. It's pleasing for those who love the South like me to have their politicians cast in such an unusual, positive light. I have not forgotten that Walter Flowers (Democrat from Alabama) whose anguish over impeachment was genuine and whose vote in favor was courageous, is such a raging supporter of George Wallace.

August 5, 1974

My chat today with Dan Schultz, the lawyer for Barker and Martinez, was pro forma. I had asked to see him originally thinking the Cubans might be included in my immunity proposal. But they got a suspended sentence, so there's no pressing reason for them to be involved. Schultz is about my age, and we have a good rapport, and I thought he did a good job of defending the burglars. He looks as if he had aged five years in the year I've known him, and he readily admits it's been a harrowing year for him.

I wanted to know if he might divulge now what other illegal "surreptitious entries" his clients might have engaged in during the period between the Ellsberg break-in in September 1971, and the Watergate break-in in June of 1972. It is publicly known that they beat up some hippies at the funeral of J. Edgar Hoover and that, as an act of fairness, they hired hippies to cause a ruckus during the Democratic Convention in Miami in 1972. But a gap remains during the fall of 1972 when a host of burglaries against anti-war and civil rights groups have gone unsolved. Also, there was a suspicious break-in at the Chilean embassy in the spring of 1972, but Senator Weicker, who knows the complete story of the Cubans, specifically denied that Barker had been responsible. Schultz confirmed this.

"It might have been some other Cubans," he said.

When I asked him about other nefarious activities, Dan smiled coyly. "It will never come out," he said, leaving the clear inference that indeed there were other episodes. The only possibility he saw of their revelation, "if there were any," would be a suit that he was contemplating against Howard Hunt to procure damages or at least a slice of book royalties from his seamy White House activities.

His read on Liddy is noteworthy. Everybody admits he's a peculiar person. He perceives himself as a spy, and a spy's code of honor demands that he never talk. He could also have refused to talk to protect the other activities of the Plumbers that had not come out. Again, I interpreted this as an additional confirmation.

Perhaps now, in the light of other monumental happenings, this is a very small piece of the puzzle, but I still think it's important that we know.

August 5, 1974, 8 p.m.

At six thirty tonight, the phone rang. My dad was on the line with an excited tone I had rarely heard in my lifetime.

"Turn on the television. He's going down the drain!"

And so it has broken. In accordance with the Supreme Court decision, the White House has released the transcript of a June 23, 1972, conversation, only five days after the Watergate break-in, that shows beyond doubt what we have felt all along but have been unable to prove: that Nixon set the cover-up in motion immediately after the break-in, directly ordering the CIA to inhibit the FBI's investigation of the break-in. He admits the tape may damage his case. The president pleads that this new revelation be put in perspective of the whole affair. If it is done so, he argued, the public will see that it does not justify his removal from office.

Tomorrow the details will be clearer. Now Charles Wiggins, the president's most eloquent defender in the House Impeachment Committee, appears on the screen. "This is not the time for the president to gather in the White House with his lawyers to discuss his defense in the Senate. It is the time for him to gather with the vice president, the chief justice, the leaders of the House and Senate to discuss the orderly transition of power from Richard Nixon to Gerald Ford. I have painfully concluded, with deep personal sorrow, that if he does not do so"—his voice broke, and he was silent for a moment—"his administration must be terminated involuntarily. Therefore, I will vote for Article One."

How I admire Wiggins suddenly. He has been brilliant in his defense, his language elegant, his points telling, his professionalism respected by all. By his efforts, he prodded the Judiciary Committee to make its case firm. And in it all, he too had been deceived. How well I remember him saying not four days ago how proud he would be to be called upon as a defender of the president in a Senate trial.

Other Republican stalwarts on the committee follow Wiggins: Wiley Mayne of Iowa and David Dennis of Indiana. Even tough-guy Charles Sandman (Republican of New Jersey) comes very close. He is going home to his district to reassess his position. In the Senate, Senator Robert Griffin, the Republican minority whip, urges resignation. Saying this would be not only for his enemies but his closest friends, Nixon should withdraw for political and personal reasons. (The president would lose his handsome pension if he were convicted, he points out.)

Several days ago, I asked Representative Pete McCloskey, an early proponent of impeachment, about this talk that the tide is sweeping inexorably toward impeachment. How did one judge a "tide" inexorably?

"That's the way it is in politics," he answered blandly.

August 5, 1974, 11 p.m.

Sirens are wailing a block away from us on Capitol Hill. A common sound. But tonight, it leads to fantasies. Are they going to get him? Has he tried something dramatic, one last desperate stab at a lifeline? The manufacture of some crisis? It is a dangerous time, these last few days or hours before a disgraced and humiliated leader relinquishes power. Tonight, the man still clinging to power must be close to derangement. Perhaps we are not as stable a society as we think. Impeachment is so little used that the process of transition tonight seems more akin to midnight knives of the Soviet Union. The rumors . . . the mental stability of the man himself . . . If he has deceived the American people and his defenders and his own family, what is he capable of now?

"He can always start a war," McCloskey had quipped.

I channel history again. As the House moved to impeach Andrew Johnson, rumors of a coup d'état were rife. Johnson had called in General Emory, commander of the Washington District, to inquire if he knew of any movement of troops in the surrounding area. Johnson had had offers of military support from several states. The story went out that a thousand troops were mobilizing in Maryland to march on the Capitol. That rumor, never verified, contributed then to the chaos in Washington.

What will be the parallel now?

78

Republican congressman Charles Wiggins, Nixon's fiercest defender, who announced his support for impeachment at the end. *Los Angeles Times*

August 6, 1974

"So it's over," the *Washington Post* proclaims today in an editorial entitled "The Guilty Plea." We have the smoking gun. In some ways, it's too easy. Something very important is getting lost in this obsession with the "smoking gun," an acknowledgment of the overall, grand pattern of abuse. Two months ago, when the Judiciary Committee had begun its proceeding, my *Post* op-ed argued for an omnibus article of impeachment akin to the eleventh article of impeachment that was brought against Andrew Johnson. But the idea went nowhere.

Now, the case is narrowed to the minutest details of the cover-up, the June 23 and March 21 tapes. This removes the lofty tone of this "grand inquest of the nation." Article Two about abuse of power and Article Three about Nixon's stonewalling on subpoenas are being forgotten. In the future, only a simple criminal act will be the standard for impeachment, rather than the abuse of powers that only a president can commit.

We're ill-served once again at this penultimate moment by Senator Howard Baker's mantra, "What did the president know and when did he know it?" A president's defense forever after will be centered on his "deniability" of personal knowledge. It's a shameful development, and it leaves me with an emptiness in the pit of my stomach.

I spent the day shuttling from one press conference after another, as congressmen lined up to switch their votes. The biggest switch came from John Rhodes, the Republican minority leader in the House, who admitted that, the day before yesterday, he was prepared to announce his decision to vote against impeachment. But someone in the White House had mercifully called him in the nick of time, warning that new damaging evidence was about to be released. He had canceled the press conference, pleading a sore throat.

The day moves quickly. Republicans are abandoning Nixon all over town. We hear that the president met with his Cabinet and said again that he had no intention of resigning. The Cabinet gave him a vote of confidence. Word also leaked out that someone in the White House compared Nixon to Captain Queeg of *Caine Mutiny* fame, the naval commander gone mad in the midst of a typhoon and relieved of his command. If he does not resign in the next few days, what other explanation can there be? Rumor has it that his daughter, Julie, is counseling a scorched-earth strategy. Bring down everybody with you, Pa. The more palatable view comes from Wiggins. He thinks the protestations not to resign are an elaborate charade to show the world that someone is still president, while behind the scenes they work out the transition of power. He thinks resignation will come in the next few days.

August 7, 1974, 3 p.m.

It's a sparkling, clear day, cool for August, with low humidity. The breeze in Washington is just right for broadcasting wild rumors. Senator Barry Goldwater (Republican from Arizona) has apparently sent a message to the White House to resign. Vice President Ford met earlier in the day with Chief of Staff Alexander Haig—was it about the transfer of power? Republican senators are meeting on Capitol Hill, trying to decide if they should send a delegation to demand the president's resignation. Rabbi Korff, Nixon's unofficial spiritual adviser, is at the White House, his red Mercedes sports car parked down the way. The *Phoenix Gazette* and the *Providence Journal Bulletin* are quoting "unimpeachable" sources that promise the president will step down later today. The source for the *Phoenix* leak is said to be Goldwater himself.

A reporter I know welcomes me to come to the White House for the "death watch." At 3:15 p.m. I check with Dad at the *Times*. The paper had Kenneth Rush, the president's economic adviser, to lunch, and he maintained the charade. The president will not resign, Rush insisted, because he sees this as a Manichaean struggle between the forces of good and evil. Rush admits only that we are dealing with an unpredictable, perhaps irrational man now. Nixon might do anything. At four o'clock I catch a glimpse of Gerald Warren, the deputy press secretary, talking to reporters in the slipway. He cannot deny

Goldwater's statement about resignation, he says, because he did not hear Goldwater say it.

These little nuances are given great weight. Someone asks Warren if he can assure us that the president will not resign before 5:30 p.m. The reporters are very interested in the report that Edward Cox, Tricia Nixon's husband, has flown in from New York. People imagine a happy family scene on television.

At 4:56 p.m., I'm standing near the ticker deep in the bowels of the White House press room when I hear a TV technician squawking that Senator Goldwater, Senator Hugh Scott, and Congressman John Rhodes, the House Minority Leader, have just entered the White House. "Did you actually see Goldwater?" "Yeah, he went through a side entrance."

I head quickly out on the lawn, and for once I'm ahead of everybody rather than on the back fringe. Within seconds the whole press corps has emptied out onto the lawn, and there are frantic questions about who actually saw Goldwater and Scott with their very own eyes. There's a time check.

Senators Goldwater and Scott with House Minority Leader
John Rhodes at the White House. *Star Collection*

August 7, 1974, 5:06 p.m.

Everything must be recorded for history. Someone shouts out, "Briefing," and the throng scrambles back into the small briefing room. Gerald Warren comes out and confirms that indeed the two senators and Congressman John Rhodes have begun to meet with the president. Questions are hurled at him:

"Jerry, will there be a statement afterwards?"

"Why not in the briefing room with the good PA system instead of out on the lawn?"

It's an ugly scene. By this time, the feeling that we're going to get a resignation today droops. Warren says the president invited the three legislators only for an "assessment." That's a different cast for the matter than earlier in the day. An assessment is different than a demand.

Shortly after 5:30 p.m., the legislators emerge and make their way through the press scrum. They keep it low key. Senator Scott of Pennsylvania, with his pencil mustache and pipe, says it was just "four old friends talking over a painful situation." But he says he told the president that the situation in the Senate was "gloomy" and "distressing." He also describes the president as "serene" and "in good spirits and in good health." This last seems to refer to Nixon's mental health. Goldwater quotes the president as saying that whatever decision he makes will be in the national interest. They claim they made no recommendations to the president about what he

85

should do. They just gave their assessment. Later that assessment is reported to be that the president might get ten votes against impeachment in the House and fifteen votes against conviction in the Senate.

All afternoon the crowd outside the White House fence has grown. They stand quietly. Many hold onto the bars of the fence above their heads. From the inside, they look like vultures.

August 8, 1974, 2 p.m.

I was tipped off that the press secretary would hold a briefing at noon, and so I rushed to the White House. Gerald Ford is meeting with Nixon at this hour, the radio in the cab blares. Just as I walked up the sidewalk, after being cleared through the gate, Ford came striding out of the door at that very moment, looking athletic and larger than I expected, accompanied by an aide and a few Secret Service men. I had to restrain myself from saying, "Congratulations," as he went past. The press room was packed. Someone said it felt like the steering room on the *Titanic*. Outside I could hear cars honking.

There were signs out there: "Honk if you think he's guilty!" "Honk because he's leaving," and "Honk if you're against immunity."

My timing had been perfect. Not five minutes after I was in the briefing room, the press secretary, Ronald Ziegler, appeared, looking haggard and on the verge of tears. His voice cracked as he announced that the president would meet with congressional leaders in the afternoon and then address the nation at 9:00 p.m. I tried to take down his words exactly in the crunch, resting my pad on a reporter's shoulder as I scribbled. When I looked up, Ziegler was gone. He had been at the podium for about ninety seconds. I went out to hail a cab on 18th Street and passed a young man who was handing out bumper stickers that read:

FORGIVE NIXON. HE SAVED US FROM WORLD WAR III.

August 9, morning

The morning broke hot and sultry with the choking heaviness of August dog days in Washington, the sun, in Stephen Crane's words, "pasted like a wafer in the sky." Nixon is on the television. His farewell dirge to his Cabinet and staff was long and rambling. At times it was genuinely moving, but not so much from what he said as from the situation: a leader more humiliated than any in American history, his fight over. One might have hoped for something noble and Shakespearean, something grand and uplifting to remember him by. But this is not a tragedy. He choked with emotion as he spoke of his father, a failure first as a streetcar motorman, then as a lemon farmer—"he sold the farm before they discovered oil on it."—and later as a grocer, but he was still a great man because he tried. And his mother was a saint, he said. He made one amusing slip along the way. "There are many good careers in America: farmers, businessmen, plumbers. . . ." No one laughed.

His free association was maudlin and embarrassing, his self-pity evoking a sloppy drunk at a bar. At other times, he was combative. Not one member of his administration had ever enriched himself by government service, not one, he professed. He did not mention the indictment of eighteen of the highest officials of his administration including three members of his Cabinet and his chief of staff. At other times, he was didactic. Never hate your enemies, he said, because then you will always lose.

Perhaps this was his final gift to his future psychobiographers. At the end, he made a point of saying "Au revoir" as if we would be seeing one another again. But it is adieu, and everyone knows it. He showed no contrition.

August 9, 11 a.m.

At this moment, the president is airborne to California. His power, fleeting down to minutes, will pass to Gerald Ford somewhere over Kansas. He will not be at the swearing in of his successor, just as Andrew Johnson, cursed with impeachment and exonerated in the Senate by only one vote, was not at the swearing in of his successor, Ulysses S. Grant. In both cases, the presence of these disgraced men would have been awkward. When it was over, he waved from the door of the helicopter and flashed the V sign. Victory for what?

On everyone's mind is whether Ford will pardon him, and if so, whether Nixon would accept the pardon, since that would be tantamount to an admission of guilt. I wonder what he might do in those last minutes of power somewhere over Kansas? Perhaps he will do something partially noble, something like declaring a universal amnesty, pardoning himself and all the Vietnam resisters at the same time. Again, I fall back on Georges Clemenceau's treatment of one of Andrew Johnson's last acts before leaving office:

"January 5, 1869: The most important event of the period has been the proclamation issued by Mr. Johnson granting a pardon and amnesty to all who have been, or are now, under judicial indictment for having taken part in the rebellion. The public has been hoping for a long time that this step would be taken. . . . The proclamation allows him to crown his career with a final act of clemency and magnanimity."

A final act of magnanimity? No, Nixon will not do that.

Good-bye and adieu. *Star Collection*

August 9, 7 p.m.

After Nixon had called upon the Almighty, and Ford did likewise several hours later, there was a terrific lightning storm and heavy rain. I could not help remembering that earlier in the year Billy Graham had said that Watergate was the judgment of God on America. Then late in the afternoon, the storm broke. I went running on the Mall, and afterward, I felt much better.

Tonight, my doldrums returned. Certainly, it is not because he is gone. I had a strong stake in that. I don't feel like reliving this day. Indeed, my mind is jumping forward to new projects, immersing myself in my new novel perhaps, to be set in the Andrew Johnson days. I'd like to forget about Washington for a while, at least this Washington. It's time to get back to small, personal pursuits.

I head back to Carolina next week.

August 13, 1974

The most interesting writing over the weekend has related to the revelations about Nixon's last days. His closest aides understood that the president had to be handled with utmost care. With the release of the June 23 tape, his chief lawyer, James St. Clair, while insisting that the tape be released, also insisted that the legal team knew nothing about it. St. Clair and General Haig then called Wiggins and showed him the transcript. Decimated, Wiggins felt betrayed and threatened to release the tape himself if the White House did not. It was suggested that the last holdouts for Nixon might want to reconsider their positions. If they did not, St. Clair threatened a Senate trial that could last six months. Meanwhile, Nixon was said to be learning toward resignation but was reconsidering because his family, especially daughter Julie, were arguing vociferously against it.

Two days before the resignation, when Senators Goldwater and Scott, along with the minority leader in the House, John Rhodes, went to the White House, General Haig pleaded with them to give Nixon an unvarnished assessment of the situation, but, at all costs, not to urge resignation. If you do that, Haig is reported to have said, Nixon might take umbrage and decide to tough it out. Kissinger is reported to have told Nixon that if he did not go, he might invite "international mischief."

Last night at a dinner party, I was bantering with Congressman Frank Thompson (Democrat from New Jersey), suggesting that Haig should get another star for his patriotic actions in the last hours. Thompson disagreed. Rather, he said, Haig's motives were devious and self-serving, and he should be busted to corporal for his disloyalty to the commander.

Meanwhile, we listened to President Ford's address to a Joint Session of Congress. As he played to his audience of old pols, his speech was pedestrian and went on far too long. Still, I found myself liking the miscues and misreading, compared to Nixon's smooth, mellifluous delivery in public and his staccato, vulgar ramblings on the tapes. There was a notable absence in Ford's speech of Nixon applause lines about the greatness of America. Later, after his inauguration in a less formal setting, Ford's voice cracked when he said,

"May our former president, who brought peace to millions, find it for himself."

Dad had a good line in his Sunday column: "Ford is everything Nixon pretended to be."

May it ever be so, for him and all his presidential successors.

Paul Conrad cartoon of Nixon as Richard II.
"O that I were as great
As is my grief, or lesser than my name!
Or that I could forget what I have been,
Or not remember what I must be now!"
Shakespeare, *Richard II*, Act 3, Scene 3

Paul Conrad's cartoon of Nixon as Richard II

"O that I were as great
As is my grief, or lesser than my name!
Or that I could forget what I have been,
Or not remember what I must be now!"
Shakespeare, Richard II, Act 3 Scene 3

Acknowledgments

MY PROFOUND THANKS YET AGAIN TO MY superb editor at
Arcade, Cal Barksdale, for his wisdom and exacting attention
to detail. As with our work together on *A Rift in the Earth*,
Cal was quick and attentive in responding to my every request
and need. He immediately saw the value and uniqueness of
the diary and pushed all the stops to ensure its timely pub-
lication. And my thanks as well to my old Carolina buddy,
Walter Dellinger, who enthusiastically rose to the challenge of
identifying the lessons of the diary and providing a broad context from his vast knowledge of constitutional law. His tren-
chant thoughts about its relevance to the current day are much
appreciated.

APPENDICES

APPENDICES

Appendix I

"Impeachment Standards," by James Reston, Jr.
Op-ed published June 30, 1974, in the *Washington Post*

In February, the staff of the House Judiciary Committee released an excellent report on the Constitutional grounds for impeachment. Replete with historical background on the English roots of impeachment law and on the Framers' intentions in the Constitutional Convention, the report concluded that criminality or indictable crime is not the sole standard for judging presidential misconduct. Stating that impeachment and criminal law serve different purposes and that impeachment was not intended as a substitute for criminal law, the report said:

In an impeachment proceeding a President is called to account for abusing powers that only a President possesses.

And yet that's the last we've heard of a general standard. Since that time, the thrust of the inquiry has been the search for the specific criminal offense. Committee members are reported to consider Book 2, Volume 5 (March 21 tape) the most important evidence against the President. Or they spend hours poring over what the President said to Dean, Haldeman, Petersen, etc. to the point where one member has color-coded his evidence books, making one man red, the other green, and so on. In this sense, the existence of the tapes and the transcripts is a disservice to the inquiry, for they have focused attention on the minutest detail and distracted from the larger picture.

Is the March 21 tape really the most important evidence there is? Why should the priority of the committee be on a conversation that took place nine months after the Watergate break-in, when it is clear that the cover-up was set in place in the days immediately after the event? Without meaning to downgrade the significance of March 21, is it any more important, for example, than the President's admitted approval of the Huston Plan of 1970 (the intelligence plan which the President claimed to have rescinded because of the practical rather than the moral or legal objections of J. Edgar Hoover)? Here is an American president saying early in his administration, as a matter of principle, that restraints on wiretapping ("electronic surveillance") and burglary ("surreptitious entry") are to be removed. Isn't that the message that spread through his administration, whether or not it was rescinded, and that set the tone and started the whole mess? Impeachment articles should begin with the Huston Plan.

In its search for specific crime the committee seems to be de-emphasizing a second standard for impeachment: "serious dereliction of public duty." This standard was defined by the House Judiciary Committee in 1970 in the proceeding against Supreme Court Justice William O. Douglas. It is this second standard that applies to the negligence of Mr. Nixon time and again in relation to the White House horrors. And this standard applies to his abuse of public trust. Moreover, did the President ever "take care that the laws be faithfully executed"?

For Presidential negligence, the Judiciary Committee should consider an omnibus impeachment article. Such an article should come at the end of specific criminal allegations, any one of which would be sufficient to remove Mr. Nixon from office. But removal is not the only point. The process is as vital as the result. And the process must go to the core of the problem: negligence—both criminal and political.

There is precedent for an omnibus impeachment article, albeit one that was put to a bad purpose. Article XI, the last of the impeachment articles against Andrew Johnson, was voted upon first, because it was thought to have the best chance of passing. As is well known, the article failed to carry by one vote.

Its author, Thaddeus Stevens, called his article "the gist and vital portion of this whole prosecution" and liked to think of it as "one and a half" articles of impeachment. The problem is that Stevens was convinced that the specific case against Johnson was weak, and so devised his article as vague, complicated and difficult to attack. He made no effort to disguise its purpose.

"Never was a great malefactor so gently treated as Andrew Johnson," he began in introducing the article. He spoke of Johnson's actions as "monstrous usurpation, worse than sedition and little short of treason." And he scoffed at the articles relating to the Tenure of Office Act already adopted by the House.

"Their tender mercies have rested solely on the most trifling crimes and misdemeanors which they could select from the official life of Andrew Johnson," he said.

But his omnibus article would be different. "If my article is inserted," he boasted, "what chance has Andrew Johnson to escape, even if all the rest of the articles should fail? Unfortunate man thus surrounded, hampered, tangled in the meshes of his own wickedness, unfortunate, unhappy man, behold your doom."

That Thaddeus Stevens was scandalously irresponsible, partisan, and vindictive should not undermine the notion of an omnibus article for this impeachment inquiry. It is vital that there be an article now—if any at all are reported out—which goes to the gist of the investigation of Mr. Nixon. If the battle is fought on the narrow ground of March 21, Congress will have made a mess of this impeachment proceeding also. And certainly, if the President were removed on such a narrow ground, the remorse of the legislators who participated in it would be as great as it was after the Johnson fiasco.

An omnibus article now would do more than accentuate negligence and void a narrow debate on who said what to whom and what was the inflection of the voice. It would establish a principle that specific criminal charges cannot be the principle of accountability. Surely the indictment of eighteen of the President's highest aides and campaign officials says something about the leadership of the Commander-in-Chief.

Likewise, an omnibus article would destroy this tawdry concept of "deniability," the notion that so long as a public official in the public trust deliberately keeps himself in ignorance of criminal activity around him, he is not culpable. As Commander in Chief, a president bears the most fundamental responsibility for the acts of his subordinates. If impeachment proceedings fail to make that point, they will have missed a vital opportunity.

Identification: *Mr. Reston is an author and lecturer in creative writing at the University of North Carolina.*

Appendix 2
The Articles of Impeachment against Richard Nixon

I. The following three articles of impeachment were approved by the House Judiciary Committee in this form:

RESOLVED, That Richard M. Nixon, President of the United States, is impeached for high crimes and misdemeanors, and that the following articles of impeachment be exhibited to the Senate:

ARTICLES OF IMPEACHMENT EXHIBITED BY THE HOUSE OF REPRESENTATIVES OF THE UNITED STATES OF AMERICA IN THE NAME OF ITSELF AND OF ALL OF THE PEOPLE OF THE UNITED STATES OF AMERICA, AGAINST RICHARD M. NIXON, PRESIDENT OF THE UNITED STATES OF AMERICA, IN MAINTENANCE AND SUPPORT OF ITS IMPEACHMENT AGAINST HIM FOR HIGH CRIMES AND MISDEMEANORS.

ARTICLE I

In his conduct of the office of President of the United States, Richard M. Nixon, in violation of his constitutional oath faithfully to execute the office of President of the United States and, to the best of his ability, preserve, protect, and defend the Constitution of the United States, and in violation of his constitutional duty to take care that the laws be faithfully executed, has prevented, obstructed, and impeded the administration of justice, in that:

On June 17, 1972, and prior thereto, agents of the Committee for the Re-election of the President committed unlawful entry of the headquarters of the Democratic National Committee in Washington, District of Columbia, for the purpose of securing political intelligence. Subsequent thereto, Richard M. Nixon, using the powers of his high office, engaged personally and through his close subordinates and agents, in a course of conduct or plan designed to delay, impede, and obstruct the investigation of such unlawful entry; to cover up, conceal and protect those responsible; and to conceal the existence and scope of other unlawful covert activities.

The means used to implement this course of conduct or plan included one or more of the following:

1. making or causing to be made false or misleading statements to lawfully authorized investigative officers and employees of the United States;
2. withholding relevant and material evidence or information from lawfully authorized investigative officers and employees of the United States;
3. approving, condoning, acquiescing in, and counselling witnesses with respect to the giving of false or

    misleading statements to lawfully authorized investigative officers and employees of the United States and false or misleading testimony in duly instituted judicial and congressional proceedings;

4. interfering or endeavoring to interfere with the conduct of investigations by the Department of Justice of the United States, the Federal Bureau of Investigation, the Office of Watergate Special Prosecution Force, and Congressional Committees;

5. approving, condoning, and acquiescing in, the surreptitious payment of substantial sums of money for the purpose of obtaining the silence or influencing the testimony of witnesses, potential witnesses or individuals who participated in such unlawful entry and other illegal activities;

6. endeavoring to misuse the Central Intelligence Agency, an agency of the United States;

7. disseminating information received from officers of the Department of Justice of the United States to subjects of investigations conducted by lawfully authorized investigative officers and employees of the United States, for the purpose of aiding and assisting such subjects in their attempts to avoid criminal liability;

8. making false or misleading public statements for the purpose of deceiving the people of the United States into believing that a thorough and complete investigation had been conducted with respect to allegations of misconduct on the part of personnel of the executive branch of the United States and personnel of the Committee for the Reelection of the President, and that there was no involvement of such personnel in such misconduct: or

9. endeavoring to cause prospective defendants, and individuals duly tried and convicted, to expect favored treatment and consideration in return for their silence or false testimony, or rewarding individuals for their silence or false testimony.

In all of this, Richard M. Nixon has acted in a manner contrary to his trust as President and subversive of constitutional government, to the great prejudice of the cause of law and justice and to the manifest injury of the people of the United States.

Wherefore Richard M. Nixon, by such conduct, warrants impeachment and trial, and removal from office.

Article One passed, July 27, 1974: 27–11

ARTICLE II

Using the powers of the office of President of the United States, Richard M. Nixon, in violation of his constitutional oath faithfully to execute the office of President of the United States and, to the best of his ability, preserve, protect, and defend the Constitution of the United States, and in disregard of his constitutional duty to take care that the laws be faithfully executed, has repeatedly engaged in conduct violating the constitutional rights of citizens, impairing the due and proper administration of justice and the conduct of lawful inquiries, or contravening the laws governing agencies of the executive branch and the purposes of these agencies.

This conduct has included one or more of the following:

1. He has, acting personally and through his subordinates and agents, endeavored to obtain from the Internal

Revenue Service, in violation of the constitutional rights of citizens, confidential information contained in income tax returns for purposes not authorized by law, and to cause, in violation of the constitutional rights of citizens, income tax audits or other income tax investigations to be initiated or conducted in a discriminatory manner.

2. He misused the Federal Bureau of Investigation, the Secret Service, and other executive personnel, in violation or disregard of the constitutional rights of citizens, by directing or authorizing such agencies or personnel to conduct or continue electronic surveillance or other investigations for purposes unrelated to national security, the enforcement of laws, or any other lawful function of his office; he did direct, authorize, or permit the use of information obtained thereby for purposes unrelated to national security, the enforcement of laws, or any other lawful function of his office; and he did direct the concealment of certain records made by the Federal Bureau of Investigation of electronic surveillance.

3. He has, acting personally and through his subordinates and agents, in violation or disregard of the constitutional rights of citizens, authorized and permitted to be maintained a secret investigative unit within the office of the President, financed in part with money derived from campaign contributions, which unlawfully utilized the resources of the Central Intelligence Agency, engaged in covert and unlawful activities, and attempted to prejudice the constitutional right of an accused to a fair trial.

4. He has failed to take care that the laws were faithfully executed by failing to act when he knew or had

reason to know that his close subordinates endeavored to impede and frustrate lawful inquiries by duly constituted executive, judicial and legislative entities concerning the unlawful entry into the headquarters of the Democratic National Committee, and the cover-up thereof, and concerning other unlawful activities including those relating to the confirmation of Richard Kleindienst as Attorney General of the United States, the electronic surveillance of private citizens, the break-in into the offices of Dr. Lewis Fielding, and the campaign financing practices of the Committee to Re-elect the President.

5. In disregard of the rule of law, he knowingly misused the executive power by interfering with agencies of the executive branch, including the Federal Bureau of Investigation, the Criminal Division, and the Office of Watergate Special Prosecution Force, of the Department of Justice, and the Central Intelligence Agency, in violation of his duty to take care that the laws be faithfully executed.

In all of this, Richard M. Nixon has acted in a manner contrary to his trust as President and subversive of constitutional government, to the great prejudice of the cause of law and justice and to the manifest injury of the people of the United States.

Wherefore Richard M. Nixon, by such conduct, warrants impeachment and trial, and removal from office.

Article Two passed, July 29, 1974: 28–10

ARTICLE III

In his conduct of the office of President of the United States, Richard M. Nixon, contrary to his oath faithfully to execute the office of President of the United States and, to the best of his ability, preserve, protect, and defend the Constitution of the United States, and in violation of his constitutional duty to take care that the laws be faithfully executed, has failed without lawful cause or excuse to produce papers and things as directed by duly authorized subpoenas issued by the Committee on the Judiciary of the House of Representatives on April 11, 1974, May 15, 1974, May 30, 1974, and June 24, 1974, and willfully disobeyed such subpoenas. The subpoenaed papers and things were deemed necessary by the Committee in order to resolve by direct evidence fundamental, factual questions relating to Presidential direction, knowledge or approval of actions demonstrated by other evidence to be substantial grounds for impeachment of the President. In refusing to produce these papers and things, Richard M. Nixon, substituting his judgment as to what materials were necessary for the inquiry, interposed the powers of the Presidency against the lawful subpoenas of the House of Representatives, thereby assuming to himself functions and judgments necessary to the exercise of the sole power of impeachment vested by the Constitution in the House of Representatives.

In all of this, Richard M. Nixon has acted in a manner contrary to his trust as President and subversive of constitutional government, to the great prejudice of the cause of law and justice, and to the manifest injury of the people of the United States.

Wherefore, Richard M. Nixon, by such conduct, warrants impeachment and trial, and removal from office.

Article Three passed, July 30, 1974: 21–17

II. The following two articles of impeachment were voted down by the committee:

Proposed Article on Emoluments and Tax Evasion:

In the conduct of the office of President of the United States, Richard M. Nixon, in violation of his constitutional oath faithfully to execute the office of the President of the United States, and, to the best of his ability, preserve, protect, and defend the Constitution of the United States, and in violation of his constitutional duty to take care that the laws be faithfully executed, did receive emoluments from the United States in excess of the compensation provided by law pursuant to Article II, Section 1, of the Constitution and did willfully attempt to evade the payment of a portion of Federal income taxes due and owing by him for the years 1969, 1970, 1971, and 1972 in that:

1. He, during the period for which he has been elected President, unlawfully received compensation in the form of government expenditures at and on his privately-owned properties located in or near San Clemente, California and Key Biscayne, Florida.

2. He knowingly and fraudulently failed to report certain income and claimed deductions in the years 1969, 1970, 1971, and 1972 on his Federal income tax returns which were not authorized by law, including deductions for a gift of papers to the United States valued at approximately $576,000.

In all of this, Richard M. Nixon has acted in a manner contrary to his trust as President and subversive of constitutional government, to the great prejudice of the cause of law and justice and to the manifest injury of the people of the United States.

Article was defeated by a vote of 26–12 on July 30, 1974.

Proposed Article on the Concealment of Information about Bombing Operations in Cambodia:

In his conduct of the office of President of the United States, Richard M. Nixon, in violation of his constitutional oath faithfully to execute the office of President of the United States and to the best of his ability, preserve, protect, and defend the Constitution of the United Sates, and in disregard of his constitutional duty to take care that the laws be faithfully executed, on and subsequent to March 17, 1969, authorized, ordered, and ratified the concealment from the Congress of the facts and the submission to the Congress of false and misleading statements concerning the existence, scope and nature of American bombing operations in Cambodia in derogation of the power of the Congress to declare war, to make appropriations and to raise and support armies, and by such conduct warrants impeachment and trial and removal from office.

Article was defeated by a vote of 26–12 on July 30, 1974.

Notes

1   **the 18½-minute gap**: The 18½-minute gap refers to an erasure of that length on a critical June 20, 1972, taped conversation between the president and his chief of staff, H. R. Haldeman. Since this was only three days after the Watergate break-in, whatever was said between the two was essential, especially if it might relate to a cover-up of evidence. The president's secretary, Rose Mary Woods, took the blame for the erasure, but her explanation was not plausible. The president's chief of staff, Alexander Haig, blamed the erasure on a "sinister force.".

1   **hush-money payments**: In the March 21, 1974 conversation between Nixon and John Dean, known widely as "cancer on the presidency" conversation, Dean lays out the full scope of the Watergate cover-up, of which he had been the "mastermind" in the previous nine months. Less remembered is the fact that the conversation was really about whether to pay the leader of the Watergate break-in, Howard Hunt, $120,000 to remain silent. Nixon did authorize the payment, acknowledging that as much as one million dollars in hush money might ultimately be needed to keep the perpetrators silent. In the case against Donald Trump, the president authorized a payment of $130,000 to a porn star, Stormy Daniels, to keep her silent about his affair with her before the 2016 election. His checks were written in the Oval Office, and the payment itself is alleged to have violated federal election laws.

4   **the Huston Plan**: The Huston Plan refers to a forty-three-page document, crafted by White House aide Tom Charles Huston in 1970, whose ostensible purpose was to coordinate domestic surveillance of "left-wing radicals," anti–Vietnam war protesters,

and counterculture dissidents. It proposed a private White House force to conduct domestic burglary, illegal wiretapping, opening the mail of "domestic radicals," and even the creation of camps to detain anti-war protesters. Never implemented in toto, it became the philosophical basis for subsequent burglaries in Daniel Ellsberg's psychiatrist's office and at the Watergate.

4 **The secret bombing of Cambodia**: The secret bombing of Cambodia was also the subject of a failed impeachment article against Nixon. The article charged that the president, personally and through aides, had submitted false and misleading statements to Congress about the bombing of Cambodia, a neutral country, in March, April, and May 1969 in violation of his duty to respect the right of Congress to "declare war, to make appropriations, and to raise and support armies." The article was defeated by a vote of 26–12. Similar worries about President Trump launching unauthorized attacks on foreign nations like Iran without the consent of Congress are being expressed in 2019.

4 **Nixon's seedy tax evasions**: Nixon's tax evasions became the subject of a fourth article of impeachment entitled "emoluments and tax evasion." The article charged two areas of presidential misconduct: improper expenditures of federal funds on Nixon's private houses in San Clemente, California, and Key Biscayne, Florida, and the failure to report certain income on his tax forms, as well as improper deductions. The impeachment article failed in the Judiciary Committee by a vote of 26–12. Charges of much larger tax deductions and emolument violations are alleged against President Donald Trump.

6 **"the Plumbers"**: The Plumbers were the "special investigations unit" formed in the wake of the release of the Pentagon Papers, ostensibly to plug leaks of classified information. In the White House, John Ehrlichman, Charles Colson, David Young, and Egil Krogh were implicated in its founding and execution. Its operatives included Howard Hunt, Frank Sturgis, Gordon Liddy, James McCord, and "the Cubans."

90 **Perhaps he will do something partially noble**: Years later, H. R. Haldeman's wife revealed that in the waning hours before

Nixon's resignation, her husband had, in fact, asked the president for a full pardon for himself and suggested he couple it with a full pardon for all the Vietnam War resisters in exile in Canada and Sweden. It would take the pressure off him, Haldeman argued. Nixon refused.